Do

YOU

Want to be a

Leader?

By Paul J Spiewak

A Personal Philosophy
of

Evaluating
Leadership
Effectiveness

and

How To Become
a
Leader

Note for Librarians: A cataloguing record for this book is available from Library and Archives Canada at www.collectionscanada.ca/amicus/index-e.html

ISBN 1-4251-0074-0

PUBLISHING™

Offices in Canada, USA, Ireland and UK

Book sales for North America and international:
Trafford Publishing, 6E–2333 Government St.,
Victoria, BC V8T 4P4 CANADA
phone 250 383 6864 (toll-free 1 888 232 4444)
fax 250 383 6804; email to orders@trafford.com

Book sales in Europe:
Trafford Publishing (UK) Limited, 9 Park End Street, 2nd Floor
Oxford, UK OX1 1HH UNITED KINGDOM
phone +44 (0)1865 722 113 (local rate 0845 230 9601)
facsimile +44 (0)1865 722 868; info.uk@trafford.com

Order online at:
trafford.com/06-1831

10 9 8 7 6 5 4 3

**"Life is like
a dog-sled team;
If you're not the lead dog,
the view never changes."**

LEWIS GRIZZARD
1946-1994
U. S. Humorist and Author
Book Title

"Lead me,
Follow me,
or
Get out of the way."

GENERAL GEORGE S. PATTON, Jr.
1895-1945
World War II General
One of the greatest military figures of all time

TABLE of CONTENTS

Preface

For fifteen years I have been a devoted member of Toastmasters International. A few months ago, a fellow member, Tennyson Tse, asked me to act as his advisor for his High Performance Leadership Project, necessary for earning his Toastmaster's Advanced Leader Silver Award.

During the course of our first meeting, he put forth his ideas for a project. After some discussion and thought, it became clear that he could accomplish all of his objectives by forming a Toastmasters Advanced Leadership Club.

Tennyson, to his credit, ran with the idea, and in less than three months, could take pride in having created and nursed the first club of its kind to the point of regular meetings and a Toastmasters International Charter.

His other advisor, Charlene Adamson, a lady who works with me, often remarked that I should write a book relating some of my experiences.

During the past few months, as work on the Club continued, I began to think seriously about the subject of leadership. Most of what has been written relates to specific areas of leadership, for example human relationships or financing. This book is an effort to view the entire subject, and then focus on those areas that I personally deem the most important.

While leadership comes more easily to some, than others, all can benefit from leadership training. The majority of today's leaders, with the exception of a few who have been painstakingly tutored, are falling short in increasing numbers. One has only to read the newspaper to note that executive after executive is indicted or resigns under fire for falsifying records, for unauthorized use of company funds, foe misleading investors, for cheating on taxes and a variety of moral offenses.

Our Federal and State government officials are no better. Rather than serving the people in this country, more and more are being caught with their hands in the till, falsifying travel records or illegally using campaign funds.

Proper training is part of the answer. Experience is another part. The problem for many is that they can't get the experience without getting the job; and they can't get the job without the experience. In the latter part of the book, I discuss how you, or anyone, can develop leadership skills and get that necessary experience.

I hope the reader of this book will enjoy this book as much as I have putting it together.

To Tennyson and Charlene, this book is dedicated to you.

"Great leaders are made, not born."

There are many well-educated and motivated people who lack the knowledge of how to lead others. So they don't assume leadership positions, or if they do, they don't do very well in them. They and others too, assume that these individuals just weren't born to be leaders.

That's really a tragedy, because our country and our people need good leaders. Corporations, associations, and athletic teams all need good leaders. Even parents must be good leaders or their families can become dysfunctional. It is hardly an exaggeration to say that our very success as a nation depends upon good leadership.

But my research shows conclusively that effectiveness as a leader depends less on some innate trait you are born with, and much more on specific principles that anyone can follow."

WILLIAM S. COHEN
1940 -
U. S. Senator & Secretary of Defense
From an article in *Network World,* December 1998

Paul J. Spiewak

"The very essence of leadership is that you have to have a vision."

REVEREND THEODORE M. HESBURGH
1917 -
President Emeritus University of Notre Dame
Influential educator of the 20th century

The Basis of Leadership

Funk & Wagnalls Dictionary
Leadership: A guiding force.

All of us are aware of so-called leaders who do not seem to lead. Why do we still call them leaders? If you think about this a bit, you realize that there are people who are called leaders because they have inherited a title, or have been appointed or elected to a particular title. The title appears to invest the holder with nothing more than the title, not with the ability to lead! Whether the title is "poobah", "sultan", "captain", "agha", "president", "king", emperor", "high-and-mighty-muck-a-muck" or anything else, the title does not create the ability to lead!

If the title is meaningless, what then can we use to determine if a leader is leading? Certainly, there have been many historical figures that were faulted for lack of leadership; and years later are extolled as having been superior. Harry Truman is a good example of this. Toward the end of his term, he enjoyed one of the lowest levels of popularity of any president before or after. Yet today he is considered by most historians as having been an outstanding president.

The fundamental question is how do we know if a leader Is leading? How do we know if a leader is effective? How do we measure or evaluate? Is there some basis by which we can compare leaders against a standard, or to each other, regardless of their place or time in history? After much consideration, I believe there is.

Every organization needs a leader. Anarchy is just not an effective system of accomplishment. Whenever anarchy exists, sooner or later organization results. Why? Because it is through organization, working together, that people make the greatest personal gains. How does a leader emerge? Can anyone be a leader? Of course, but every organization not only needs a leader, but needs an effective leader,

Every organization also needs a vision, a mission or purpose. The founders of any organization, by necessity had to have a picture of what the organization would be. They needed to have a mission or purpose for that organization, before it could become viable.

Big corporations often extol both their vision and their mission(s); but whether publicly stated or not, any organization never would have been formed without some underlying purpose.

Unfortunately, the mission is often inadequate. A common misconception of a business mission is "to make a profit." This is not a true mission because it is too generic. It is equivalent to organizing a charitable organization "to help the sick." The mission needs substance, and if a leader arrives, the leader's main function is to flesh out that mission, so that everyone, employees, customers and the outside world know why that organization exists. For a charitable or social organization, it is just as important. The March of Dimes (National Foundation for Infantile Paralysis} was originally formed in 1938 by President Franklin D. Roosevelt, himself a victim of polio, to search for a cure for this often-deadly disease. With the development of the Salk and Sabin vaccines in 1954, this huge organization had completed its mission. Did it close the door? Obviously not, as it is still around today. The leaders redefined the mission to adapt to changing circumstances, and this organization has spread its influence even more widely. Its fundamental mission, to help people, still exists, but the wider mission has been redefined to provide assistance to other afflicted persons, and now deals with handicapped children, premature births and other medical conditions.

It is almost tautological, i.e. to define leadership with its own word, to state that the fundamental, most basic characteristic of a leader is to lead. By "lead" we mean: to define the mission, to clarify it to the point where everyone understands why the organization exists, and in what fundamental direction or purpose the organization will pursue.

A person assuming the reins of power should have a very clear concept of the end purpose of the organization; and must either have or create a clear and clearly defined mission (purpose), for that organization, before he/she can lead effectively. The mission or purpose, thus clarified, may be ill-advised. It may be unattainable. That's not the point. However misguided a mission may be, it defines the conditions for which the leader ultimately can be held responsible. Without that clarity of purpose, it is impossible for a leader to operate effectively.

It should be clear that there is a distinct difference between management and leadership, although many historical figures have possessed both talents. The legendary Peter Drucker said it best: *"Management is doing things right; leadership is doing the right things."*

Without that vision, without that purpose, the leader is powerless. He/she has no idea where to lead. It is rather like Lewis Carroll's *Alice in Wonderland* in this exchange with the Cheshire Cat:

`Cheshire Puss,' Alice began, rather timidly, as she did not at all know whether it would like the name: however, it only grinned a little wider.' Alice, went on. `Would you tell me, please, which way I ought to go from here?' `That depends a good deal on where you want to get to,' said the Cat. `I don't much care where--' said Alice. `Then it doesn't matter which way you go,' said the Cat.*

Thus, we conclude, that without a clear purpose, leadership is impossible.

Anyone aspiring to leadership must first have a vision and then transfer that vision into a mission or purpose. Failure to have a mission simply gets back to our friend Alice.

When you don't know where you are going, any road will do!

Having a clear purpose, while being the basis for leadership, is simply not enough. The accomplishment of that mission, assuring that the mission will be achieved, and the manner in which it will be achieved are the bases by which the effectiveness of that leadership can truly be judged and evaluated.

The Triple S of Leadership

Once having that clear purpose, then is up to the leader to devise a plan to enable, encourage, assist, cajole, threaten, whip, persuade, influence, convince, plead, sway, argue, convince, facilitate, coax, wheedle, entice, sweet-talk, inveigle, flatter, or force, those who follow to exert efforts to help in the fulfillment of that clearly stated mission.

How the leader works to achieve that mission provides the clues to his/her effectiveness. There are many ways to judge a leader and effectiveness of leadership. One of the objectives dealt with in later chapters is to create a meaningful scale by which a leader's effectiveness can be evaluated.

Leaders have different backgrounds, different styles, different viewpoints, different education and different experiences, all which play a part in what the leader does. Despite these differences, my belief is that a leader's effectiveness can be judged by employing these three criteria, which I call the Triple S of Leadership:

Strategy – in moving the organization toward fulfillment of the mission

Succession – the provision the leader makes for continuing the movement toward fulfillment when he/she (the leader) leaves or is incapacitated.

Style – the way the leader leads, i.e. the tactics employed. Style also includes those character traits of the leader which tend to influence others. Many of those traits ultimately are condensed into one characteristic, the ability to command respect.

These elements provide the key to determining leadership effectiveness. They can be applied to judging the effectiveness of any leader: past, present or future. Other factors may be considered, but these three are those which are critical both to leadership and leadership evaluation.

Any system of leadership selection or leadership evaluation ultimately succeeds or fails on these three considerations.

Even though there have been thousands of articles written about the things that make up leadership quality, every one of these eventually distills into one or more of these three.

As a leader, you need to have the vision and the mission before you can lead effectively. As a case in point, consider the political situation in 1948. Harry Truman, a Democrat, suffering from very low standings in the popularity polls, was running for re-election. Tom Dewey, an extremely effective Republican New York prosecuting attorney, was considered a "shoo-in." Dewey's campaign emphasized the need for effective government. Truman, on the other hand, attacked the 83rd "do-nothing" Congress as the source of the problem. The Republicans, without a vision or a mission, except to defeat Truman, were overwhelmed by Truman. The Democrats not only won the presidency, but Truman's coattails swept in a Democratic majority in both the House of Representatives and the Senate.

Strategy

Funk & Wagnall's Dictionary
> Strategy: A plan or technique of achieving some end on a broad scale, as distinguished from tactics

If you listen carefully to the promises and statements made during presidential campaigns, you quickly realize that the speaker is simply presenting a vision. Promises are made to entice you to share that vision without specifying how that vision is to be carried out.

Unfortunately, and quite frequently, the strategy does not conform to the mission. This is especially true in the political arena. After the horrible events of 9/11, for example, President Bush went on television, and stated a new mission: "to capture Osama Bin Laden, dead or alive!" His popularity soared, because the American people could agree with that sentiment. BUT! What was the strategy that followed? Was it an all-out pursuit of Bin Laden? Was it a negotiation with Pakistan to put forces in the field to find and apprehend him? Suddenly, it seemed, Bush lost sight of Bin Laden and created a new mission. He caused us to invade Iraq in search of weapons of mass destruction. When those weren't found, he created still another mission: to bring a democratic government to Iraq. Certainly, the public was confused as to what the mission was. There was no strategy outlined to end the conflict. There was no strategy to find Bin Laden. There was no strategy to locate the missing weapons of mass destruction. Without the strategy to complete any of these missions, is it any wonder that Bush's popularity ratings tumbled?

The business world is quite different. A business is floundering, losing money, or on the verge of bankruptcy. A new chief executive officer is brought in to "turn the company around." Three or four months later, the new CEO is forced out. What happened? What went wrong?

There are several answers. First, it is possible that the CEO did not create a workable strategy for solving the problem(s), or created a strategy that was unacceptable to the board, or, perhaps, even worse, did not create a strategy at all.

It is a fundamental facet of leadership that the leader not only shares the vision and the mission but has an effective strategy to carry it out. Without a cohesive effective strategy, how can the purpose of the organization be achieved?

The essence of leadership is to employ a strategy that directly relates to carrying out the mission. If that strategy is not readily understandable, or if that strategy is deemed to have little chance of success, then it is almost certainly doomed to failure.

The fundamental reason for defining a strategy is to complete the mission, or if that is not possible, at least to move the organization toward completing the mission. Surely, everyone can understand that a mission might take longer than one leader's tenure or even one person's life.

If there is any single rule of effective leadership, it is that the mission must be clearly defined, and that the leader devises and supervises the attainment of that mission by means of the stated strategy.

John F. Kennedy, created a national vision in which the United States would "put a man on the moon within ten years." The mission was to develop the technology to make this possible. Very few really believed that it could be done in that time frame, because his term in office had only three years remaining. Yet he anticipated that his successor would carry on that mission to completion. To that end, he convinced Congress to pass legislation forming the National Air & Space Administration to continue the effort after he was gone.

Not every leader has the opportunity to create the vision. Many leaders do not even have the freedom to define the mission. While both the vision and the mission may pre-exist, any leader, to be effective, must have the freedom to create his own strategy

The employment of an effective strategy is what truly makes a leader effective. This is not a new concept. Most people familiar with the book of Exodus in the Old Testament would agree that Moses was a titan when it came to leadership.

His vision was clear: Eberu (non-Egyptians) people living in freedom in a land of plenty. His mission was clear: Lead the Eberu (later translated to Hebrews) people to freedom in the Promised Land. Even the strategy was clear: Convince Pharaoh to "let my people go" and depend upon the Lord to show them the way to the Promised Land.

As a leader, Moses was highly effective. He had a vision which defined his mission, which in turn dictated his strategy.

"Leadership can be thought of as a capacity to define oneself to others; in a way that clarifies and expands a vision of the future."

RABBI EDWIN H. FRIEDMAN
Noted author
Reinventing Leadership
Friedman's Fables

Here is a real life example.

In 1951 I was hired as the manager of a local fuel oil distributor. At the time of employment, the company was in financial trouble. Fuel oil, in those days, was comparatively inexpensive, costing approximately eight cents per gallon, wholesale. Customers were billed at an average price of ten-and-a-half cents a gallon. Out of that two-and-a-half cents gross profit, the company had to pay the costs of distribution, sales and administration. Sales and administration costs were quite small, but a simple analysis showed that the cost of delivery was too high to make a profit.

Even though my mission was unstated, it was understood that I needed to do something to restore the company to profitability. At the time, several distributors functioned by using automatic deliveries under a "degree day" system. My previous experience and knowledge of this system was the major reason I was hired...

I proposed a simple strategy:

1. Convert all customers to automatic delivery, except where emergency deliveries were required.

2. Accurately track each customer's usage to insure that when a driver stopped to make a delivery, he could pump the maximum amount of fuel into that customer's tank.

The theory behind this was that by maximizing the number of gallons delivered to each customer, the truck would need to make fewer stops and thus become more productive. This was done during the first winter season. Results were better, but not good enough. Under the old system, we had delivered five million gallons during the season, using fourteen trucks. At the end of the first season using the degree day system, we had managed to pump six million gallons using only twelve trucks. While it was a significant improvement, we needed to do better.

There was an alternative system, used very successfully by a few large firms... Instead of calculating degree days, they employed a staff of "tank stickers." Each sticker had a regular route, going into a neighborhood and "stick the tanks" of the company's customers. This process involved sticking a measuring rod into the tanks to see how many inches of oil remained. Whenever a sticker found a low tank, a truck was sent to fill ALL the tanks in the neighborhood. The theory here was that by minimizing the miles needed to drive the truck, the truck could maximize the number of customers serviced, and thus become more productive.

One evening, in what surely was an epiphany, I suddenly realized that we were asking the wrong question. One system was designed to maximize the amount of oil pumped into each tank, without regard to the distance between tanks. The other system was designed to fill every tank in an area, and thus avoiding traveling excess distance, but without regard to the number of gallons pumped into each tank. The correct question was "How do we maximize the amount of oil delivered by each truck?"

The answer was actually fairly simple. A hybrid system was designed and implemented, with the express strategy of maximizing the amount of oil delivered. The next season, the company was restored to profitability by pumping nine million gallons with only ten trucks. Thus in only two years, the amount of fuel pumped had grown by

80% while simultaneously reducing the number of trucks (and drivers) by 40%. The effect amounted to a 70% cost reduction in the cost of delivering each gallon!

This case demonstrates the duty of the leader to carry out the mission in an expeditious, rational and successful manner. Anything less detracts from the leader's effectiveness.

While there are many qualities associated with leadership, there is no escaping the fact that a leader who fails to either complete the mission or move the organization to the completion of that mission, is ineffective.

In that sense, Albert Einstein, arguably the greatest physicist in history, set his mission to define the Unified Field Theory. His personal evaluation of his own work was that he had failed because he was unable to complete that mission. We recognize him today, not only as a great physicist, but also as a great mathematician and a spokesman for the scientific community. Yet, by his own evaluation, he failed as a leader.

Former President Jimmy Carter is another example, Most people would probably agree on his high moral character and his services as a humanitarian, but the strategies he employed as president to carry out his mission failed.

Strategy is the definition of practical steps to achieve the organization's mission. A leader, who does not employ such a strategy effectively, fails as a leader. Bear in mind that this is not a character evaluation but simply an evaluation of that person as a leader.

**"Our strategy is how we
cope
—how we measure
and weigh
what is to be said
and when,
what is to be done
and how,
and to whom
and to whom
and to whom"**

CHERRIE MORAGA
1952 -
Hispanic American Feminist Author
This Bridge Called My Back

Strategy and Objectives

Strategy is a complex topic. Because it may involve several disparate items, there is a need for the leader to break it down further. These subsections are often called "Objectives."

For example, I am sure that every one would agree that the vision of every president of the United States is of a well-protected land of crime-free, contented, materially-satisfied people who have unlimited opportunities for education, access to quality health care and opportunities for cultural development in a peaceful world.

There are clearly different goals in this vision. Every president we have ever had wanted to accomplish all of these, and every president knew that he could not possibly accomplish all of these.

As a result, this vision was translated into a mission by each president. The mission was an attempt to clarify and state which of the elements in the vision were to be achieved and to what degree. The stated mission was to accomplish those facets of the vision which the president believed were possible to be achieved.

The strategy that followed became a goal of those individual items in order of priority. The effectiveness of any president became directly related to his ability to implement the steps, and the tactics to accomplish that purpose.

Since 1948, for example, starting with President Truman, every president declared his intention to secure peace in the Middle East. At times, this goal was a priority of the moment, but there were always other things that seemed to take precedence.

The reality of setting a strategy, defining the specific objectives in order of priority, always provides a blueprint of what a leader hopes to accomplish. That is, by definition, the strategy. Each leader must either confirm an existing strategy or redefine the strategy in accordance with his own thinking.

On a presidential scale, it may be that several items have "top priority," because with the size of the United States government, individual segments may operate simultaneously on several fronts. Typically, each president has both a foreign mission and strategy and a domestic mission and strategy.

Dwight Eisenhower, applauded as an administrator, saw this picture perhaps better than any other president. His vision initially was focused on the war in Korea. His mission, and promise to the people of this country, was: **"I shall go to Korea, and I shall end the conflict."** Unlike many other presidents, within days after his election, he kept his promise, went to Korea and settled the conflict. This effort consumed half of his first term, but the American people, in appreciation and gratitude, overwhelming re-elected him to a second term.

After the Korean War ended, Eisenhower, with his military experience, realized that a major difficulty in conducting the war in Korea had been the lack of a good, high speed road system in the United States. There had been too many delays and difficulties transporting both men and materiel across the country. As a result, he formulated a new vision of a network of high speed highways criss-crossing the country. He sold this new mission to Congress as the first step in his strategy. Surely, all would agree with the enormous payoff in creating the Interstate Highway System we enjoy today.

Strategy is not only in government. In the business world, owner-operated businesses rarely have a well-formulated strategy. That is the major reason why 95% of them fail in their early years. It is also why even those who remain never grow or progress.

The mission of the chief executive of a public corporation is to maximize and increase profits to insure that those who financed the company get a bigger and better return on their investment.

While the vision and the mission are both apparent, strategies differ widely, not only in type, but also in priority.

It is the leader's duty and responsibility to define a strategy to make and improve the company's profitability. That is the mission. Further, the leader needs to define or accept a strategy to make that mission a reality. That defined strategy becomes a series of steps, for each of the eight objectives, in priority order.

"Objectives have to be set in these eight key areas:

1. Marketing,
2. Innovation,
3. Human Organization,
4. Financial Resources,
5. Physical Resources,
6. Productivity,
7. Social Responsibility,
8. Profit Requirements."

PETER F DRUCKER
1909-2005
Eminent Teacher, Author & Consultant
From his 1973 book
Management, Tasks, Responsibilities, Practices

Other than the objective of profit requirements, these apply to almost all organizations, but the priority of the remaining objectives may differ from organization type to organization type.

While there is no practical way to prove it, my belief is that the failure to set down the priorities, and to follow through, is the reason for the failure of most leaders. In my own case, I have failed in twelve of my nineteen entrepreneurial ventures. In retrospect, it is obvious that in each case of failure, it was primarily a result of a failure to recognize the need for literally documenting the vision, the mission and the strategy. Without that vital tool, I failed because I had not specified the relative priorities of these objectives.

As a designer of software, for example, I created a magnificent system of accounting control for the legal profession. As an executive of a public company in the computer service bureau business, in the 1960s, my team created the programs necessary to perform this type of work. A single salesman, in the space of two years, signed up more than 5,000 lawyers in New York City, including a dozen of the twenty largest firms in the world, to use this system. The net profits of this (my) division exceeded that of the total company. This led authoring several sections of the *Manual for Managing the Law Office*, published by Prentice-Hall in 1970.

Setting up my own company, after the service bureau business had been replaced by "in-house" mini-computers, I re-wrote that system. Because of the advance of technology, there were drastic changes in computer language and systems design. I poured my resources into it and finally produced what I considered to be a truly great product. Unfortunately, and stupidly, I used all my resources in creating the product with no funds allocated for marketing. Meanwhile, IBM, with one of the best marketing teams ever created, was peddling a vastly inferior system with great success. I had failed to set priorities among my objectives, and the world failed to beat a path to my door.

This is not an unusual situation. Failure to properly and effectively allocate limited working capital is, perhaps, the greatest single reason why the great majority of new businesses fail. It is also true, it should be noted, that many fail, not because they don't properly allocate capital, but simply because they did not have enough to start in the first place.

Strategy and Planning

Can you imagine the Continental Congress creating the United States of America without any documentation? Can you imagine building a skyscraper without written plans? Why is it then that so few organizations are created and run without definitive and written plans?

The typical small business owner when asked for his business plan is prone to tap his forehead and say "It's in here!" Paraphrasing the movie producer Sam Goldwyn: ***"A plan that is not written down isn't worth the paper it's written on."***

Aside from the memory factor, there are many good reasons for writing a plan. Each of the eight objectives has to be analyzed and coordinated with the others. Specific goals need to be established, with both timing and financial requirements. Invariably, when creating a plan, there will be some goals which cannot possibly be met without downgrading others. The plan ultimately is the defined strategy for achieving the purpose and for fulfilling the mission.

The most difficult part, for almost any organization, tends to be financial. Finances directly affect every other item, be it marketing, administration or production. Inadequate working capital is probably the single most important reason that companies fail. Another is improper use of capital, usually due to poor planning!

A few years ago we witnessed a shake-out of the electronics industry, the so-called "dot-com fiasco." There were many companies flush with cash and ideas. In order to raise that cash, they were required to submit documents to the Securities & Exchange Commission (SEC) specifying what and how that money was to be used. Despite that SEC requirement, many companies failed. Even those who survived watched as their stocks plummeted. "Why," you might ask, "if they had the money and the plan, did this happen?" The underlying reason is that the planning was invalid. Just because you make a plan, no matter how detailed, is not a guarantee that it will occur.

A plan not only has to be created, it has to be watched, carefully nurtured and adjusted as conditions change. It is not something to be finished and put into the drawer. The plan represents the day-to-day tactics necessary to fulfill the strategy. The strategy fulfills the mission. The mission brings the vision to reality. Here are two examples, one positive and one negative.

When Thomas Edison set out to create the electric light bulb, he was faced with many problems. Chief among these was finding a filament that would not only emit a satisfactory amount of light, but one that would not burn out too quickly. He tried a succession of materials, but none seemed to work. In fact, he failed more than 10,000 times. A friend of his asked him one day, if he wasn't discouraged by all these thousands of failures. "Not at all", Edison said. ***"I've eliminated more than 10,000 different materials that will not work."*** Edison had a testing plan. He kept careful notes in order not to repeat tests on the same material.

Adolf Hitler had a plan to conquer all of Europe into a single country and empire which would last 1,000 years. His plan didn't work, and the "1,000 Year Reich" lasted less than ten years,

The plan is the starting point. As experience dictates, the plan gets revised. In 1991, I was the driving force behind the creation of a new business. An elaborate plan was drawn to raise capital. We started with our vision. Then we defined the mission, followed by the strategy, listing and explaining each revenue-producing aspect. The plan included spreadsheets, graphs and narrative, projecting the theoretical first ten years. The plan was good enough to attract some outside investors, and the business began, attempting to follow the plan. Recently, in cleaning out some files, I found a copy of the original plan. Absolutely nothing in the original plan was ever implemented successfully! Nothing! Digging further, I found the plan for the year 2000. We are doing everything in that plan, and a whole lot more. Indeed the business that we had in 2000 represents less than half of the things we do and offer today, six years later.

If a business seeks investors through sales of stock, the SEC (Securities & Exchange Commission) has very strict rules. One of the chief requirements is the approval of a document called a "Red Herring" which includes the purpose (mission), outlines the company's business (the strategy), and how it intends to use the capital raised (the plan).

While planning is essential to carrying out the strategy, bear in mind the hierarchy. Successful execution is the only real test of leadership effectiveness. Starting from the top, here's the way it should be
1. Vision
2. Mission
3. Strategy
4. Objectives
5. Planning (Tactics)
6. Implementation

"A community is like a ship; everyone ought to be prepared to take the helm."

HENRIK IBSEN
1828 -1906
Influential Norwegian Playwright
"The Father of Modern Drama"

Succession

Succession is a difficult subject for most leaders because it is inherent for any leader to believe that no one else can lead as well as he/she can. It is also difficult because most people do not think of themselves as prone to disease, illness or even death.

The wise leader must first accept the principle of fallibility, and get past the ego problem. He/she must recognize that mortality is part of life. Further, that the success of the strategy in fulfilling the mission depends upon designating and training a successor.

In some cases, there is an orderly procedure already in place to designate a successor in the event the leader cannot function. The United States Constitution, for example, provides for many possible eventualities to insure that no matter what dire circumstances occur, that there is a designated party or method of succession.

In war-time, no matter the branch of service, if the leader is killed or wounded, everyone in a unit knows who is in line to take command. There is a complete lack of ambiguity, because even if there are two equally ranking officers, the one whose commission was received earlier becomes the leader.

The case for orderly succession extends back in time. The eldest son of the tribal chief became the leader when the old leader fell. As civilization advanced, feudal leaders adopted the same system. In almost all monarchies, the oldest prince became the king, or the oldest daughter became queen. The transfer to the oldest son, by

*"The final test of a leader
is that he leaves
behind him, in other men
the conviction
and the will
to carry on."*

WALTER LIPPMANN
1889-1974
U. S.Writer, Photographer, Journalist,
Political Commentator

primogeniture, was extended to the point where the oldest son became the owner of the family farm, and younger sons were forced to go out on their own.

Bear in mind that this was not necessarily a bad arrangement. Dividing a kingdom among princes would necessarily diminish the power of each. Similarly, dividing a farm among children could reduce the size to uneconomic portions. In times when large families were prevalent, both kingdoms and farms would be lost.

The true leader specifically selects and trains a successor to carry on after the leader passes on. In today's corporate market, it is not unusual to have several such candidates at the same time, leaving it to the Board of Directors to make the final selection when the time arrives,

In the Middle Ages, a master craftsman would take on an apprentice, who gradually learned the craft, became a journeyman, and ultimately a master craftsman in his own right. In many countries today, the cloak of leadership passes within the family: North Korea, Cuba, and Saudi Arabia, to name a few. Sometimes it is not acceptable to those being led, with violent results, such as in Haiti.

In United States political life, cases of family control of a specific job are rare, although there have been a number of specific exceptions. John Adams and John Quincy Adams (father & son), both were presidents as is the case with the George Bush family. There also was the case of William Henry and Benjamin Harrison (grandfather and grandson). Those who were born before WWII, surely recall the legacy of Adlai Stevenson, who over a period of years had a strong record of service to the nation, starting with the grandfather (Adlai

Stevenson I) serving first as a Congressman and later as the twenty-third Vice President, and as a presidential candidate after the end of Cleveland's presidency in both 1896 and 1900.   His son, Lewis, served as Illinois Secretary of State, and Adlai II serving first as Senator from Illinois and then as an unsuccessful Democratic candidate in both campaigns against Dwight Eisenhower.

There are also many political cases where a son follows his father into the Senate or the House of representatives.

Unlike politics, corporations do not quite follow the same rules. All of us are aware of the many small family-owned businesses, where the passing mantle of both ownership and leadership to the next generation is fairly common. In public corporations, succession is primarily in the hands of the Board of Directors. In some cases, the expected successor is given the title of "heir apparent." There are many large corporations where the leadership is passed down to other members of the family; Disney and Du Pont are two well-known examples. Fairly often, it is reasonably common to find one, or more, executives within the organization being trained to take over the helm, upon the demise of the leader.

One of the major, and most often neglected, responsibilities in any organization, is to train a person or persons to be able to continue the mission, to carry out the strategy in the event of the leader's demise. The reason is probably psychological, because preparing someone to "take over" implies the passing of the trainer. This process can be painful, but if done well, can literally save the mission from failure. A notable case in point is the assumption of the presidency by Harry Truman, after

Franklin Roosevelt died. Truman was totally unprepared to carry on, and was not even aware of the existence of the atomic bomb project. It is fortunate for the American people that he was a quick learner, giving the order to drop the bomb only four months later.

In general, there are two ways in which a successor can be trained. The first is an educational process, during which the leader passes on information, and at the same time he/she makes sure that the designated successor is trained in the details of the leader's job.

Much more powerful are specific illustrations and leadership <u>by example</u>. I remember after being discharged from the Army, I went to work in my father's and grandfather's factory. They made sure that I was trained in every department and could earn a basic wage (piece work) in each department, before I was moved on to the next position. I clearly remember the time when I was aggravated at the previous operator because the material she passed on to me was slightly "off," but still in passable condition. My annoyance was expressed rather loudly and crudely. Suddenly, there was a hand gripping my shoulder. It was my father. He said, *"Son, there are two kinds of people in this world: those who are big on peanuts; and those who are big on elephants. Don't be big on peanuts!"*

Another example is inherent in this old story, The Tale of the Wooden Bowl. It goes like this:

A frail old man went to live with his son, daughter-in-law, and four-year old grandson. The old man's hands trembled, his eyesight was blurred, and his step faltered. The family ate together at the table, but the elderly grandfather's shaky hands and failing sight made eating difficult. Peas rolled off his spoon onto the floor. When he grasped the glass, milk spilled on the tablecloth. The son and daughter-in-law became irritated with the mess. "We must do something about my father," said the son. I've had enough of his spilled milk, noisy eating, and food on the floor. So the son and his wife set a small table in the corner. There, Grandfather ate alone while the rest of the family enjoyed dinner. Since Grandfather had broken a dish or two, his food was served in a wooden bowl. When the family glanced in Grandfather's direction, sometimes he had a tear in his eye as he sat alone. Still, the only words the couple had for him were sharp admonitions when he dropped a fork or spilled food. The four-year-old watched it all in silence.

One evening before supper, the father noticed his son playing with wood scraps on the floor. He asked the child sweetly, "What are you making?" Just as sweetly, the boy responded, "Oh, I am making a little bowl for you and Mama to eat your food in when I grow up." The four-year-old smiled and went back to work. The words so struck the parents so that they were speechless. Then tears started to stream down their cheeks. Though no word was spoken, both knew what must be done. That evening the husband took Grandfather's hand and gently led him back to the family table. For the remainder of his days he ate every meal with the family. And for some reason, neither husband nor wife seemed to care any longer when a fork was dropped, milk spilled, or the tablecloth soiled.

When training someone to be a successor, the old saw "Do as I say, not do as I do" carries no weight. The leader, as a mentor, a teacher and advisor, must constantly illustrate to the successor-to-be, the proper methods and actions.

Over the past fifteen years, I, with the loyal and dedicated assistance of my wife, built a very enjoyable business. Recent medical problems staring me in the face are a testament to my vulnerability. For the last two years, I have been gradually transferring responsibility to others, both employees and out-sources. The job is not complete, but the day is approaching when regular business operations no longer depend upon me.

Unfortunately, even though this is a family-owned business, there is no one in the family who is ready, willing and able to take over. Both the size and unique nature of the business work against that. After considerable thought, it became apparent that rather than looking for a successor, the business would be better served by breaking my functions into components, and then simply transferring one component at a time. In some ways this is much easier and better. Current employees have all been given additional duties, allowing each one to grow. Each has been pleased with the new responsibilities and my daily chores get lighter each passing month.

This orderly preparation to solve the matter of succession is a paramount consideration of leadership. A leader may leave the organization for many reasons, including personal ones that have no relation to the organization. Sudden incapacity of a leader has occurred again and again in history, sometimes with disastrous results, even to triggering internecine conflicts, destruction of the organization and even wars.

Failure to provide an orderly means of succession OR failure to train a future leader is, in plain terms, the abdication of a major function of effective leadership.

"If your actions inspire others to dream more, learn more, do more and become more you are a leader.

JOHN QUINCY ADAMS
1767- 1848
President of U.S. Constitutional Convention
U.S. Senator, U.S. Secretary of State,
Foreign Ambassador
4th President of the United States

Style

Every person is endowed with a style, a way of doing things. There are some people we just don't like, because they "rub us the wrong way." Others, we tend to like, even when we disagree with them. What is the main difference between one person and another, or one leader from another? Why do we try hard to please one boss, and not another? Why are we attracted to some people and repelled by others?

It's a matter of style and other factors that influence your thinking, such as: physical appearance, speech patterns, facial expressions, eye contact, proximity and body movements.

Approval of a leader's style makes absolutely no difference in leader effectiveness. While the leader may want to be liked, the essence of leadership is to perform the mission, not popularity. Confusing leader popularity and leader style with leader effectiveness is sadly quite common. It most likely is the single most important reason we have so many poor legislators.

At some point, the leader must ask, "Am I accomplishing the mission?" It is the mission that is of paramount importance, not the continued tenure of the leader, although, many times these can be defined as one and the same.

If we look at some of the well-known world leaders in history, you will readily see that Josef Stalin's mission was to make the Soviet Union the most powerful country in Eurasia. By the end of World War II in Europe, he had largely succeeded. Was he popular? Hardly!

"The leaders who work most effectively, it seems to me, never say "I."   And that's not because they have trained themselves not to say "I."   They don't think "I." They think "we"; they think "team."   They understand their job to be to make the team function. They accept responsibility and don't sidestep it, but "we" gets the credit.... This is what creates trust, what enables you to get the task done."

PETER F DRUCKER
1909-2005
Eminent Teacher, Author , Consultant

In the course of building the Soviet Empire, Stalin executed, depending on which report you believe, between twenty and sixty million of his own people. In contrast, and within the same time frame, the benevolent King Christian X of Denmark was held in very high regard, but failed to keep his country out of the Nazi orbit.

If all this is true, how can we equate the effectiveness of a leader with how he is perceived? Leaders can be benevolent or despotic, cruel or gentle, demanding or forgiving or one side of many such opposites. Yet, whether we like the leader or not, there are individuals in history that we instinctively believe were great leaders. Surely, all who believe in the Old Testament would regard Moses as a great leader. He carried out his mission to lead the Hebrews out of the land of bondage, and he led them for forty years. He provided for leadership succession in the persona of his brother Aaron. Even though he was sometimes harsh and demanding, he was respected. Even though he smashed the golden calf and castigated the entire assemblage, he was respected.

There you have the solution to style. Regardless of the style, to be effective, the leader must be respected. Respect cannot be bought, it must be earned. This matter of respect, is the essential difference between the true leader and the "wannabe." A leader must earn the respect of those he leads as a leader! You may have contempt for the way he conducts his personal life, but still respect him as a leader. The epitome of this type of thinking can be found in the now famous "We shall fight on the beaches" speech after the disaster and rescue at Dunkirk during World War II. Here is an extract from that speech, which literally mobilized the entire English people:

"We shall go on to the end,
we shall fight in France,
we shall fight
on the oceans and seas,
we shall fight
with growing confidence
and growing strength
in the air,
we shall defend our island
whatever the cost may be,
we shall fight on the
beaches. We shall fight
on the landing grounds.
We shall fight in the fields,
and in the streets,
we shall fight in the hills
We shall never surrender!"

(SIR) WINSTON CHURCHILL
1874-1965
British Prime Minister during World War II
House of Commons June 4, 1940

This is a prime example of a brilliant leader, highly regarded as a war-time leader, admired by many for his talents as a painter, a speech writer, an author and a historian, who was not respected as a post-war leader. Why? Apparently, the British public was simply tired of wartime austerity. Despite his political fall, he was subsequently elevated to knighthood and continued to hold the respect of most Americans. Evidently, there was a clash in the perception by the British people who viewed him as a highly respected wartime leader, but believed he would be inadequate in peacetime.

Clashes can easily occur between a figure's private and public lives. Many presidents have had mistresses and retained their popularity with the public as a president, with others bemoaning the low moral standards and bad examples being set by the holder of this powerful position. The fundamental point is that despite the moral peccadilloes, the public retained its respect for the president as a leader, not as a private individual.

Sometimes the difference between appearance and reality may be covered by a feeling of respect for the individual. Surely, this was true of President John F. Kennedy. At the time he was running for the office and in his speeches after he was elected, the media constantly talked about his "charisma." It was done so frequently, that it was almost as if the entire country was brainwashed. Certainly, he was an excellent communicator, had a wonderful sense of humor, and portrayed himself in an exemplary manner. People respected him and admired his style. Yet, he failed to accomplish almost all of his goals, and it was left to Lyndon Johnson, who took over after Kennedy's assassination, to put the Kennedy program though Congress.

"On the night of the tenth of May [1940], at the outset of this mighty battle, I acquired the chief power in the State, which henceforth I wielded in ever-growing measure for five years and three months of world war. At the end of which time, all our enemies having surrendered unconditionally or being about to do so, I was immediately dismissed by the British electorate from all further conduct of their affairs."

(SIR) WINSTON CHURCHILL
1874-1965
British Prime Minister during World War II
Excerpt from his book *The Gathering Storm*

To put this in better perspective, as soon as the war was over, Churchill lost his position as prime minister. He was still respected as perhaps the greatest wartime leader in history, but somehow could not carry that respect forward. His party lost the election and his resignation was forced. On the facing page, is an excerpt from his book The Gathering Storm, published in 1948, three years after the war ended.

While I emphasize respect, style, is much more. Without respect, the leader cannot lead. The way the leader earns that respect is comprised of many elements.

These elements of style include, but are not limited to: ethics, persistence, communications ability, human relations, innovation and decisiveness. Not every leader has to have a full measure of these qualities, but they are representative of the values that leaders evidence to gain respect. For example, there have been many tyrannical leaders who have had loyal followers despite severe failings in ethics.

Adolf Hitler is an example of this, as all would agree, to be charitable, that his ethics were highly questionable. Yet he commanded the respect of his staff, because the entire German command at that time was sympathetic to the same ethical level. On the other hand, he relied on his staff and within the body of the ruling body, he commanded respect, at least until two years before his demise.

*"Ethics, too,
are nothing but
reverence for life.*

*That is what gives me the
fundamental
principle of morality,
namely that good consists
in maintaining, promoting,
and enhancing life,
and that destroying,
injuring, and limiting life
are evil."*

ALBERT SCHWEITZER
1875–1965
Doctor, Philosopher, Author,
Humanitarian, Theologian

Ethics

It is a sad fact that we appear to be besieged by leaders in all fields who are unethical or even worse. Daily, we read about corruption of politicians, immorality among the clergy, and misuse of money by business executives. Television commentators report each new malfeasance with glee, but even journalism has had its share in recent years: falsifying stories, propaganda disguised as news, revealing secret information to the detriment of loyal citizens.

Several years ago, we encountered some problems with the employees of a Convention & Visitors Bureau who was hosting one of our company's conferences. Several months later, I had the opportunity to meet with one of the top executives of that bureau. He initiated the conversation because he wanted us to return and hold another conference at his location. I explained what happened. We discussed it for a while. Then he nodded, and said. "No matter what happened in the past, we want to do the right thing." He corrected the problem, and we've been back to run a conference at his location four more times since, and have agreed to return again.

Doing the right thing is sometimes difficult. It is often unpleasant. Sometimes, it is even expensive. In my own business, our refund policy is fairly strict, although we believe it to be fair. Those who are denied refunds often disagree; and sometimes, if circumstances so indicate, we bend the rules.

"Reputation is what other people know about you. Honor is what you know about yourself."

LOIS MCMASTER BUJOLD
1942 -
Canadian born
Award winning U.S. science fiction author

"Real integrity is doing the right thing, knowing that nobody's going to know whether you did it or not."

LOIS MCMASTER BUJOLD
1942 -
French & US actress & television talk show host

By doing the "right thing" in 2005, we refunded 14% of our total revenue. Did it hurt? In the short run, perhaps, but as we examined each one, we realized that most of the time, and in most cases, we got the money back when the customer rebooked. Aside from the money, we have gained enormous respect and good will in the industry. People enjoy doing business with us. They want to advertise with us. In fact, what the refund policy has done is earned their respect.

Shady or marginal operators do not earn respect. The rot in a bad apple eventually surfaces. Some will think me naive. Some try to take advantage. Yet honor and integrity, the two are almost synonymous, have been with us since the beginning of man.

Honor, as acknowledged by philosophers and religious figures since the dawn of history, is not what you owe to others. Rather, honor is what you owe yourself.

A few years ago, I went to a stockholders meeting of a locally based national corporation. The Chairman made a rousing speech, telling us how great the business was going and urging us to invest even more in the company. Three weeks later, the company announced it would fall short of its earnings estimate, not only for the current quarter, but also for the year. I, and I'm sure many others, bit the bullet. We took our losses, but the distrust of the chairman has lingered. Many of the shareholders who took losses as a result of the false statement would never again invest in a company involving that chairman.

A more recent example is the dry cleaning establishment I have been patronizing for 27 years. Picking up my suit one day, I could see that the front button had been smashed, most likely by the pressing machine. I asked that a new button be sewn on.

They insisted that there was a $5 charge. "But, you broke the button", I protested. The owner pointed to a small sign on the wall which said, "Not responsible for buttons." I paid the $5, but I ask you, "Was that the right thing?" Was that honorable?" I paid the $5, but I took my $1,000 a year dry cleaning business elsewhere.

Most of us have had similar experiences, where the person we dealt with failed to do the right thing. Did they really gain by it? As a leader, how do you expect to earn the respect of those you depend on, if you are not honorable?

Honor is the essence of human interchange. Without honor there can be no real respect. Without respect, a leader ultimately will fail.

"Failure is not an option"

GENE KRANZ
1933 -
Air Force Officer
Research Director McDonnell Aircraft Corporation
NASA Procedures Officer
Flight director, Mission Control, Apollo 13

*Message to the ground crew in Houston during the
critical earth-to-moon decision loop.*

"Nothing in the world can take the place of persistence.

Talent will not; nothing is more common than unsuccessful men with talent.

Genius will not; unrewarded genius is almost a proverb.

Education will not; the world is full of educated derelicts.

Persistence and determination alone are omnipotent."

CALVIN COOLIDGE
1872 - 1933
30th President of the United States

Persistence

"Throwing good money after bad" is a common expression describing the foolishness of spending more on something which has little chance of success. The trick is obviously in knowing when to give up. Quite often, a minor change can alter the whole aspect. How many times have you tried to do something, like opening the lid of a tight jar? You twist with all your might, and you can't move it. Do you give up? Most people do not. Next, you try running hot water over the cap, on the theory that the heat will make the cap expand more than the glass. You try again. Again, you fail. You start banging the edge of the cap with the back of a knife. You fail again. Do you give up? Now, try prying up the edges of the cap with a small screwdriver. You hear a slight hiss, and the lid screws off easily. <u>At what point do you give up?</u>

In our business, we started a program of memberships with the idea of increasing advertising sales for our magazine. We set up a membership program with minimal benefits, charging $50 per year for membership. If an advertiser spent $1,000 or more, we offered a free membership. At the end of one year we signed up 100 members, about half of which paid the $50 and the rest received it free. The total amount of advertising was virtually unchanged. The net value of the program to us was at most $5,000. It was hardly worth the effort. Did we give up? No! What we did was rethink the entire situation. What were we trying to accomplish? The fact is that nobody is going to spend $1,000 on advertising they don't want for something that is nominally worth $50.

What was the solution? Change the program! How? The membership fee was raised and our advertising rates were raised by 10%. A benefit was added offering a 10% discount on ads for members only! The difference in response was miraculous. After five years, membership is $399 with an extensive list of member benefits. Membership fees now are a major source of company revenue.

This phenomenon of "looking through the wrong end of the telescope" is all around us. Here are a few examples.

The U. S. Post Office

The greatest expense in operating the U. S. Post Office is, unquestionably, labor. Well over half of that labor cost is for delivery of mail, both residential and business. The most significant way to reduce that expense would be to eliminate deliveries. Yet, the Post Office charges you if you want a box at the post office to pick up your mail. They should turn the telescope around by giving you a box at no charge, and charging you for home delivery.

The Telephone Company

One of the high cost items for the telephone company is that cost of printing directories. Yet, if you want an unlisted number, saving the telephone company paper and printing costs, you are charged extra.

Ford Motor Car Company

This case is peculiar, but at least it produced additional revenue. When Ford first produced the Mustang, in 1964, the standard car had a front bench seat. One of the more popular options was bucket seats, for which there was an additional $79 charge.

When Ford examined the wonderful sales results, they took note that 99% of all purchasers had selected the bucket seat option. The following year, 1965, in addition to the planned increase, Ford made bucket seats standard, and added another $79 to the price.

The sequel is about the buyer who preferred the original bench seat. Ford solved this problem neatly by calling it an option and then, you guessed it, by charging an additional $79.

Federal & State Safety Regulations

We have been conditioned almost since birth to accept the color green as a sign to go, and red as a signal to stop. Why then, are the rear lights of your auto showing red when the car is moving forward?

Industrial Salespeople

Statistics clearly indicate that 80% of all industrial sales occur after the eighth sales call. Statistics also show that 80% of all industrial salespeople give up if they haven't made the sale by the third call.

These few examples offer anyone who is, or aspires to be, an effective leader. It offers an opportunity to examine and re-evaluate his/her approach, when faced with failure. Persistence is not a headlong flight, but if Method A isn't working, the leader should look for method B, and persist! Quite often, this means changing the tactics employed, but not the strategy. The effective leader persists, but remains aware and flexible. The Mission stays intact. The Objectives are intact. The Strategy stays intact. Only tactics are changed.

"Communication requires both a sender and a receiver.

If either is missing, there is no communication."

CLAUDE E. SHANNON
1916 - 2001
American Mathematical Engineer
President of Bell Telephone Laboratories
Founding Father of the "Electronic Communications
Age
Inventor of Information Theory

Communication

Almost every member of the animal kingdom has some ability to communicate by both sound and body language. Birds fly in formation, bees fly in swarms, fish swim in schools; and with sounds or body movement undecipherable to us, they change direction as a unit, flee or even disperse,

Man has this ability also, but man is unique with complex spoken language as well as the written version. Unfortunately, too many in our society neither communicate clearly nor properly.

The ability to communicate well is not inherent in human make-up. Communication skills have to be learned. Many studies show that the single most important factor for success is the ability to effectively communicate.

It should be obvious for anyone desiring a position of leadership, that he be able to communicate well. A leader cannot become a success in life until he learns how to communicate with power and effectiveness!

People who rise to the top of their businesses or organizations and who gain prominence in their professions share one common trait - they are people who learned how to communicate effectively! Remember, if you don't know how to speak with power and confidence, you are putting yourself at a severe disadvantage professionally - with implications for your financial well being.

"I learned that a great leader is a man who has the ability to get other people to do what they don't want to do and like it."

HARRY S. TRUMAN
1884 – 1972
U.S. Senator & Vice President
33rd President of the United States

A young man who was such a poor speaker, handicapped with both dyslexia and stuttering, that he was rejected from college. His teachers gently advised, because of his difficulty communicating, to avoid any career dealing with the public. This young man was Winston Churchill; the very same Churchill who went on to become one of the greatest speakers of all time. This is the same man, through the power of his spoken word, rallied his nation and the Free World to defeat Hitler.

Any individual can improve his relationships, better his career and increase his financial potential by becoming a better communicator! Study after study shows that communication skills are the key to advancement. Every study shows that as an executive reaches middle-management and beyond, the primary criteria for advancement are communication and motivation skills rather than basic job performance.

Putting it bluntly, a leader cannot lead if he is unable to communicate what his subordinates should do. Communications are vital for every business, indeed for every relationship.

It is important to understand that communication is a two-way street. You need both ends for a successful communication. It is difficult to motivate people without communication, and when you communicate as a leader, you need to sound like a leader.

"I suppose leadership at one time meant muscles, but today it means getting along with people."

INDIRA GANDHI
1917 – 1984
3rd & 6th Prime Minister of India

Dealing With People

Dealing with people is an extension of communication. Sometimes the communication is by action, rather than words, but the effects can be just as devastating. People in positions of authority are often oblivious to the effect their communications, both in language and actions, have on subordinates. Sometimes the effect on people is the reverse of what was intended. Here are several "real life" examples out of my own experience.

Case 1, The Distribution Company

Receivables were growing and the boss didn't like it at all! He fired the A/R Manager, and promoted someone else to the position. The entire training consisted of a terse instruction, "You call these people and tell them to pay up." Instructions were followed, with little result. The new manager was fired and someone else was promoted, with the same result. The boss called a meeting of everybody in the office and started off with saying "You people should bend down and kiss my feet for giving your families bread to eat." Was the A/R problem ever resolved? Frankly, I don't care. I was out of there three days later and found a job with a competitor.

Good leaders strive for good communication with their subordinates. They strive to motivate. In this case, fear of losing a job was the first reaction. The second reaction, on my part, was that I no longer wanted to work in a place that cared so little for its employees.

*"When dealing with people,
let us remember
we are not dealing with
creatures of logic.
We are dealing with
creatures of emotion,
creatures bustling
with prejudices
and motivated
by pride and vanity."*

DALE CARNEGIE
1888-1955
Super-Salesman, Author, Educator
Creator of *Dale Carnegie Self-Improvement Course*

Case 2, The Service Company

Heading up a new division, I was promised (in writing) ten percent of annual profits generated by the division. Each month, a statement was issued by the home office showing the profit status for the month and for the year to date. Things were going very well, as I had unearthed a new source of revenue. At the end of the twelfth month, I eagerly opened the year-end report to see how much extra money I had earned. Much to my surprise and dismay, the year-end report showed that I had lost money! What the company had done was to allocate a sum equivalent to 25% of my annual revenue for "home office overhead." My protests were in vain and I was gone three weeks later. In the process they lost a manager who went from zero to more than a half-million in sales in the first year. Meanwhile, they had difficulty finding a replacement and closed the operation the following year.

Well, the carrot was dangled and I chased it. Corporate greed never pays, and this is a classic case. In fact, the company clearly lacked integrity, and to me it was no place to have a career.

Case 3, The Manufacturing Company

I was a star! After years of living with production and inventory control problems, I found a solution! The company manufactured some 8,000 products in eleven product lines. At the time of my arrival, overall inventory turnover was an atrocious 1.5 turns. In addition, customer dissatisfaction with delayed deliveries was seriously hurting the business.

"In these matters the only certainty is that nothing is certain."

PLINY THE ELDER
23 AD - 79 AD
Roman Scholar. Philosopher, Scientist

By applying my education and researching the problem, I devised a new statistical sales forecasting system, learned to program a wired computer, created the necessary program, went through six months of testing, arrived at a workable solution; and tested it on the smallest product line (only 110 items) for six months. The system not only worked, It worked even better than anyone (including me) had anticipated. Turnover on this one product line had risen from .5 to 12, a 2,400% improvement! Customers, used to shipment delays of 90 to 120 days, were getting deliveries in 3 days. Stale inventory dissolved and sales increased.

Two days after the study on the effectiveness of the system had been circulated to the Board of Directors, I was called into the president's office. The president welcomed me with a big smile and compliments. He told me that he had just received the year-end financial reports and that it was clear that my efforts had saved the company more than a quarter million dollars. Strangely, he added, one quarter million is the total profit the company earned that year. "Even though this is not salary review time", he said, "I'm putting you in for an immediate raise for achieving these fantastic results." Then came the kicker: "We're giving you a raise of $5 per week."

What would your reaction be? If you were in my shoes, what would you have done? Was this an expected consequence? As a result of this magnificent gesture, my employment was voluntarily ended, as soon as I could find another position.

In each of these cases, Management failed to get the expected results. Is this usual?

*"If I always appear
prepared,
it is because
before entering
an undertaking,
I have meditated long
and have foreseen
what might occur.*

*It is not genius
where reveals to me
suddenly and secretly
what I should do in
circumstances unexpected
by others;
it is thought and
preparation."*

NAPOLEON BONAPARTE
1769-1821
French General, Politician, Emperor

Dealing With the Unexpected

The Law of Unintended Consequences holds that almost all human actions have at least one unintended consequence. In other words, each <u>cause</u> has more than one <u>effect,</u> including <u>unforeseen effects</u>. In the twentieth century, it became known as the Law of Unforeseen Consequences.

This law is the basis of criticism of many government programs. Surely, all of us are aware of "side effects" of prescription drugs. Another example was the levying of an import quota on steel to protect the American steel companies and steelworkers. The unintended result was steel became more expensive for U.S. automakers, whose prices became less competitive with foreign automakers, to the detriment of the automobile industry and auto workers.

After the Exxon Valdez oil spill, most states enacted laws placing unlimited liability on tanker operators. The net result was the movement of oil shipments to "fly-by-night" operators with leaky ships and questionable insurance.

History is loaded with many examples. Who would have predicted a tax on tea would result in the Boston Tea Party and ultimately the American Revolution? Similarly, Rosa Parks' refusal to go to the back of the bus triggered the "equal rights" social revolution.

Increased airport security after 9/11 has resulted in inconvenience and delays that have impacted airline business. For many, myself included, a drive of 500 miles is now more convenient than flying.

Two "classic" examples contributed to the bankruptcy of Pan-American Airlines. In an attempt to improve flight bookings, the leaders issued a directive that service was to be discontinued at airports where less than 40% of the traffic originated there. The unexpected result was that service to Las Vegas, one of their most profitable items, was dropped. The other Pan-Am classic came after the takeover of National Airlines. National had a successful service called the Florida Shuttle, with daily inexpensive flights between Miami, Orlando and Tampa. It was so successful, that it was rare for a plane to fly with empty seats. The edict from Pan-Am, however, dictated that any route that could not increase its traffic by 10% in the next 90 days would be discontinued. As it was impossible to increase 10% over 100%, the service was discontinued shortly thereafter.

Another classic was the 1962 Chevrolet II, with outstanding foreign sales. The compact muscle car battle caused Chevrolet to introduce a high-powered engine, accompanied by a name change to "Nova". Unfortunately "No Va" in French, Spanish and Italian means "No Go", and off-shore sales plummeted.

One of the important qualities for a leader is to be able to assess the side effects of any decision. Few lawmakers examine the realistic consequences of legislation before they vote for it. Few presidents examine the consequences of policy changes.

Few inventors ever look at the downside of their inventions. Email, for example, has resulted in a flood of garbage, lies, ads, swindles, scams never before encountered. Dynamite, invented for peaceful purposes, became a tool for warfare safe-blowing. Russia experienced an upsurge in automobile thefts. Car owners installed car alarms.. Thieves simply waited until an owner opened the car and then shot him before stealing the car. Car owners then gave up on alarms and installed security systems, making it impossible to hotwire. Thieves simply resorted to carjacking, which resulted in more injuries and deaths of drivers.

The obvious fact is that actions designed to be beneficial can have disastrous consequences, because of an inability to "think it through." A major function of an effective leader is to be able to assess the ramifications of any new policy or action.

As a leader, you will sooner or later have a situation where a grievous error has been made, either by you or by one of your subordinate. How do you handle it? Here is where honesty and integrity can help! First, if you made the mistake, "'fess up!" Admit you made an error – Yes! Even to your subordinates and your superiors. Get it out of the way and start taking action to first, correct the situation; second, to prevent a recurrence. Remember that refusal to "fess up" was the cause of the downfall of Richard Nixon.

If one of your subordinates made the error, it is still your fault! One of the penalties of leadership is that while you get the glory, you also get the blame. To quote President Harry Truman: *"The buck stops here."* In the process of taking the blame, you, as the leader, must also determine how to handle the subordinate. Regardless of the circumstances, to the outside world (and that Includes your superiors), it is your fault. For many leaders, a condition of this type is an opportunity to establish a solid following. Those leaders who refuse to admit they are wrong or try to blame a subordinate simply do not earn the loyalty they need to perform well.

"The leader must know, must know that he knows and must be able to make it abundantly clear to those about him that he knows."

CLARENCE B RANDALL
1891-1967
Presidential Medal Of Freedom Dual Recipient
President Inland Steel Company
Chairman Council of Foreign Economic Policy
Presidential Counselor to DDE, JFK & LBJ
Author: *Making Good in Management*

At one point in my career I was considering joining forces with another consultant who I had been working with on one project. He made a suggestion that I thought was unworkable. I said, "Stanley, you're wrong." With that, his faced turned red. He slammed his hand down on the table and said "I may not always be right, but I am never, never wrong!" It was his client. We did it his way. It didn't work. We never worked together again.

Another time, I was engaged in a cooperative effort with NCR (National Cash Register Company) to install a specialized application computer system in a remote location. I had designed the system and written the programs. NCR sent a pleasant young man, Frank, to install the hardware. The programs were put through three test runs. On the third test run something went wrong. I told Frank that we had a machine problem, and to call me when he had fixed the problem. Six hours later he called me to say that he had pulled everything apart, had checked everything, carefully reassembled everything and was ready for another test.

Another test had the identical problem. We decided to check each program step to find the error. About a third of the way through, I suddenly realized what the problem was, and it was clearly my fault and my fault alone. "Frank". I said, "I think It's time I bought you a beer!" He looked at me, nodded, and replied, "This is going to cost you more than one. If you hadn't been so positive, I would have said it was software all along. But, six extra hours!"

Frank was a nice young man, and after the third beer, he turned and said, "At least you admitted it was your fault as soon as you found the problem." We were friends for years.

"The defeats and victories of the fellows at the top aren't always defeats and victories for the fellows at the bottom."

BERTOLT BRECHT
1898-1956
German Dramatist, Stage Director, Poet
The Threepenny Opera

Leadership Evaluation

The old chief died and his son appointed by the tribal elders to become the new chief. He was confident on the outside, but uncertain as to his ability to perform.

He called upon the Wise Man of the Woods (WOW) for advice. The WOW listened to the young man, and then led him over to the fire. There was a boiling pot of water, and the WOW dropped in a carrot and an egg. After a suitable time, the WOW fished out the carrot and placed it in a wooden bowl. Likewise, he fished out the egg and placed it in a second bowl. Then, in the still hot water, the WOW dropped in a handful of coffee beans and let the water come to a boil once more. He then poured the water into a third bowl.

Turning to the young chief, the WOW handed him the first bowl and asked him to feel the carrot. "It's soft", he said. The WOW then handed him the egg and told him to break it. The young chief peeled the egg. "It's hard", he said. Then the WOW asked him to sip the coffee. The young chief smiled as he tasted the coffee with its rich flavor and aroma. Then he asked, "What does this all mean?"

The WOW explained that the carrot, the egg and the coffee had each faced the same adverse circumstances, the boiling water. He pointed out that each had reacted differently. The carrot, which was strong and hard before adversity, had become soft and weak. Conversely, the egg which had been so soft and fluid it had required a shell to protect it, had become hardened and no longer needed the shell. The coffee beans were totally different. They had changed the water!

"The problem is not that there are problems.

The problem is expecting otherwise and thinking that having problems is a problem."

THEODORE ISAAC RUBIN
1923 –
U. S. Psychiatrist, Columnist, Playwright

"Which one will you be?" asked the WOW. "When hard times come will you lose your strength and will, and become limp like the carrot and lose your strength? Will you be like the egg, and become hardened to the needs of your people? Or will you be like the coffee bean that changes the adversity, the boiling water that caused the pain? If you are like the coffee, when things grow worse, you grow better. You change the situation. When the hour is the darkest and trials are their greatest, will you, can you, elevate yourself to another level? How do you handle adversity? Are you a carrot, an egg or a coffee bean?"

It may well be that the surest test of a leader is how the leader acts when things are going badly. No matter how successful a company is, there are times when outside events, totally beyond the company or leader's control, can create adverse circumstances.

The classic case is Johnson & Johnson's reaction to the Tylenol Crisis of 1982. Tylenol, manufactured by J & J was the leading over-the-counter painkiller, controlling almost 40% of the market. J & J was faced with a devastating situation when seven people died in Chicago after taking Tylenol capsules. It was determined that the product had been laced with cyanide after it had reached store shelves. Public announcements were made warning people against use of the product. Sales plunged.

J & J acted swiftly even though they knew they were not responsible. They took the responsibility of protecting people as their first concern; and at a cost of more than $100 million, they removed every container of the product from store shelves, nationwide.

Then J & J took four steps to re-introduce the product.

1. They created new tamperproof packaging.

2. They offered $2.50 discount coupons.

3. They reduced prices by 25%.

4. They hired more than 2,200 people to make sales presentations to the medical community.

The crisis passed, and despite many new products on the market, including new J & J products, Tylenol today has a dominant position in the over-the-counter painkiller market.

Compare this with the Exxon crisis in 1989. After the massive eleven million gallon oil spill in Prince William Sound, which was clearly their responsibility, Exxon delayed responding to the problem. Additionally, Exxon never took responsibility, thus proving to the world that it had absolutely no regard for the environment, no regard for the tourism business, and absolutely no regard for the fishermen whose livelihood was destroyed. Ultimately, the cost to Exxon was in excess of $2 BILLION, and a tremendous loss of public goodwill.

In most organizations, the immediate result of adverse circumstance is usually financial. What ineffective leaders fail to realize is the public loss of confidence in the long run will probably cause a greater financial loss.

Heads of charitable organizations are considered effective if a fund drive produces an increase. College presidents are largely hired for their ability to attract donations and endowments. Politicians appear to be totally attuned to donations. In big business, the measure of a leader seems to be profits, with publicly owned stock prices suffering huge decreases because of a shortfall of penny or two in earnings per share.

Yet, money is not really a test of leadership. A recent survey indicates that "more than half of the six million middle managers in the U.S. and Canada fail to achieve the expectations of those that hire them." These middle level leaders suffer from a serious lack of management support and seldom given a clear mission by their leaders. They are, as a group, mostly untrained and rarely are they skilled in people management.

If we go back to the fundamental requirements for effective leadership: Strategy, Succession, and Style; you can easily understand why so many are unsuccessful.

Some years ago, when I was involved in the service bureau business, our night shift manager quit. The obvious choice was Danny, our lead daytime operator. Danny was eager for the promotion and we needed the job filled. He got the job, and we moved another daytime operator to take Danny's old job. Another day time operator was hired. Unfortunately, Danny was neither management oriented nor trained. He had absolutely no skills in handling people. Demands on him for many of the supervisory skills he needed simply were not needed in his prior position. At the same time, it rapidly became clear that the operator who had been moved up to take Danny's old job did not have the ability to maintain a machine schedule.

"The transition from the industrial age to the information age is a huge shift. In all of human history, there have only been two other socioeconomic revolutions of this magnitude: the move from hunting and gathering to agriculture and from agriculture to industry.

We know that leadership is very much related to change. As the pace of change accelerates, there is naturally a greater need for effective leadership."

JOHN P. KOTTER
Harvard Business School Professor
Distinguished Leadership Authority

Strictly because of lack of training, we wound up with two problems instead of one.

This condition, as indicated by the majority of failures in middle management, is a general non-recognition of the importance of proper training. It is a denial of the need to prepare for succession, the most neglected of the Three S' of Effective Leadership.

One of the reasons for the success of the specialized military attack forces, such as the Commandos and Rangers, is that:

1. The mission is clear. The plan has been reviewed. The strategy is clear.

2. Succession is not a problem because every man knows every job. If any individual falters, any one in the group can pick up where he left off.

3. Style is a result of standardized training, because style is nothing more than tactics. The same tactics are taught to everyone in their basic training.

The requirements for effective leadership are straightforward. The Triple S' system offers not only a system of evaluation of others, but points the way toward development of your own skills and accomplishments as an effective leader.

While you may want to assign different weights to each of the Three S', for illustrative reasons let us use a simple scheme where: the <u>strategy</u> towards accomplishment or advancement toward completion of the mission has a value of 50 points; <u>succession</u> has a value of 30 points, split between the succession procedure and successor training; and the balance of 20 points to <u>style</u>.

Using this technique will permit us to form a picture of effectiveness for any leader, past or present. This technique can also be used for evaluating the <u>relative effectiveness</u> of past presidents and world leaders.

This process is an attempt to quantify leadership effectiveness, an area heretofore strictly subjective. You have the right to change the number of points for each of the factors, as long as you do it uniformly throughout the mix. It should also be noted that there may be major disagreements between individuals as to the actual assignment of point values. Nevertheless, it is important to go through the process for you to understand and for you to appreciate the technique involved. Comments are solely the opinion of the author. Feel free to disagree.

Sample Leader Evaluations

The principles outlined in the foregoing chapters were used as the basis of evaluating a few famous leaders. Evaluations and scoring are strictly the opinion of the author. You are invited to re-evaluate these leaders on the basis your own opinions. Additionally, when you have completed this section, it is suggested that you make your own list of leaders you admire and have admired. Then, apply the same technique.

Before you begin, you may want to change the way each of the three factors are scored. Originally, the factors were equally weighted. In our personal experiences, we were exposed to many leaders whose style we deplore, yet who were effective in achieving THEIR individual missions.

Whether or not you agree with the mission has no bearing on the evaluation. The fundamental criterion for evaluating the effectiveness of a leader is whether that strategy achieved the mission and fulfilled the purpose. Thus, style was down weighted. I clearly recall one boss who, on taking control; his first action was to open up a dozen bank accounts in various parts of the city. His standard practice was to write checks on one account and deposit that check in a second account. The following day, he would write a check on the second account and deposit it in a third account. He continued this process through the various accounts. This occurred in the 1950s, when it still took the Federal Reserve two to three days for inter-bank check clearing.

By "kiting" this way, he could easily pay bills and take advantage of the common 2% early pay discounts. He was earning 50% interest (annual rate) on the original check. Eventually he had to cover the first check, but he had two or three weeks to cover the original check with new customer receipts. Ethical? Hardly! It borders on illegality. I challenged him for acting in a dishonest manner. He answered that as long as he could get away with the practice it was legal. Further, as far as he was concerned, it was legal, it was ethical.

My style rating for him is zero. Yet he accomplished what he set out to do and achieved his goal. As his follower, I felt uncomfortable. I stayed because I needed the job, but left at the first opportunity, because I simply did not trust him. My reasoning was that if he could cheat the banks and get away with it, I ultimately would be a victim. His style was faulty, but he still managed to fulfill his mission.

You can appreciate that in this case, style was not a major factor. There are many cases, however, where style is critical to achieving the mission. In a scientific laboratory, for example, you cannot force scientists to create. In a similar way, there are situations where leadership style is critical. In a military campaign, communication, a style factor, is often a determinant of ability to complete the mission.

The same dilemma exists in assigning values to the element of Succession. For governments in most of the world, and certainly in the United States, a succession procedure is built into the law. The tradition of a two-term limit for the presidency was established by our first president, George Washington. Franklin Roosevelt violated this tradition and went on to not only a third term, and was re-elected to a fourth. Many citizens were not pleased.

Only six years after his death the 22nd Amendment to the Constitution was fully ratified, imposing a two-term limit. Only sixteen years later, in 1967, the 25th Constitutional Amendment was ratified containing a major revision in the presidential succession procedure.

The factor that is not built-in to the succession procedure, is the training of the successor. If the mission is fulfilled and completed, it doesn't matter whether there is a trained potential successor or not. However, most organizations are designed to continue long past the demise of the present leader. Having a trained successor in the wings is extremely important. Indeed, if one examines small businesses, which are responsible for most of the jobs in the country, it is a rare business that has a succession plan in place, much less a specific person trained for that position. While many directors and ex-directors of public corporations have told me that "Succession is the most important element of leadership;" it is difficult to credit this factor as more important than completing the Strategy.

Fulfilling the mission, however it is defined, is the specific charge for any leader. He can have the most wonderful style, have a thoroughly trained successor, but if he does not fulfill that mission, or at least set the organization on the course to fulfilling that mission, he has obviously failed. For this reason, some readers may decide that the strategy element in evaluation is worth far more than the 50% I awarded to it.

Our evaluation scale, was applied to a few examples of 20th century leaders. Here are the results.

*"Do not wait for leaders.
Do it alone,
person to person."*

----

*"It is not how much we do,
but how much love
we put in the doing.
It is not how much we
give, but how much love
we put in the giving."*

MOTHER TERESA
1910 - 1977
Beloved Humanitarian

Mother Theresa

a. Strategy (maximum 50 points).

Anyone who reflects upon the life of this saintly lady would agree that her mission to help the poor and the sick was clear. Her entire life was devoted to that effort. Despite severe setbacks, she persisted in carrying out her mission.

Rating: 50 points.

b. Succession (maximum 30 points).

1) Process (maximum 15 points).

Mother Theresa gets some credit for training many people to carry on her work, although there was no plan to appoint a single successor.

Rating: 5 points.

2) Training (maximum 15 points).

The effort continues where she established her base of operations. Regretfully, she did not train anybody to extend her operation.

Rating: 5 points.

c. Style (maximum 20 points).

While a hard taskmaster, and with a reputation for assertiveness, this lady commanded word-wide respect, attention and admiration.

Rating: 20 points.

Total Rating: 80 points.

"You must be the change you wish to see in the world."

"You must not lose faith in humanity. Humanity is an ocean; if a few drops of the ocean are dirty, the ocean does not become dirty.

Freedom is not worth having if it does not include the freedom to make mistakes."

MOHANDAS K. (Mahatma) GANDHI
1869 - 1948
Indian ascetic & nationalist leader

<u>Mohandas "Mahatma" K. Gandhi</u>

a. Strategy (maximum 50 points).

Gandhi had two missions, the first to liberate India from Great Britain without violence, the second to achieve a united India, Clearly his strategy resulted in a successful completion of the first, but religious prejudices in his own population defeated him in the second. Was it possible? Probably not!

Rating: 40 points.

b. Succession (maximum 30 points).

1) Process (maximum 15 points).

Regretfully, no provision was made.

Rating: 0 points.

2) Training (maximum 15 points).

While associates, particularly Jawarahal Nehru who later became prime minister was influenced by him, he was not given any specific training.

Rating: 5 points.

c. Style (maximum 20 points).

Gandhi endeared himself to the world with his campaign of non-violence. In that role he was an outstanding figure, still revered by millions.

Rating: 20 points.

Total Rating: 65 points.

"Let me assert my firm belief that the only thing we have to fear is fear itself - nameless, unreasoning, unjustified terror which paralyzes needed efforts to convert retreat into advance."

"Men are not prisoners of fate, but only prisoners of their own minds."

FRANKLIN DELANO ROOSEVELT
1882 - 1945
Asst. Secretary of the Navy, Governor of New York
32nd President of the United States

Franklin Delano Roosevelt

a. Strategy (maximum 50 points).

Elected to four terms as U. S. President, FDR had several missions. The first was to lead the U.S. out of a depression. He was only moderately successful until WWII production did the job. His next mission was to complete the war successfully. Although he died only three weeks before "V-E Day," and four months before "V-J Day," it was clear that the Allies would ultimately win, and FDR's mission would be successfully completed.

Rating: 40 points.

b. Succession (maximum 30 points).

1) Process (maximum 15 points).

The U. S. Constitution provides.

Rating: 15 points.

2) Training (maximum 15 points).

FDR failed to inform or train all three of his Vice Presidents. Harry Truman, taking over upon FDR's death, did not know about the A-bomb, which was used to bring about Japan's surrender.

Rating: 0 points.

c. Style (maximum 20 points).

The public loved FDR, not only for his Fireside Chats, but mostly for his sense of humor. His opposition felt that he was "too full of himself" and viewed himself as a king.

Rating: 10 points.

Total Rating: 65 points.

There's only one difference between the Israelis and the Arabs. They want to kill us, and we don't want to die.

We can forgive you for killing our sons. But we will never forgive you for making us kill yours.

GOLDA MEIR
Israeli Foreign Minister 1956-1965
Israeli Prime Minister1969-1974

Golda Meir

a. Strategy (maximum 50 points).

Meir's missions were to protect Israel and to achieve peace. She accomplished the first, but tragically failed to achieve the still unattained, perhaps impossible goal of peace with the Palestinians. She led the country during the Yom Kippur War in 1973 and left political life the following year.

Rating: 40 points.

b. Succession (maximum 30 points).

1) Process (maximum 15 points).

Israeli Constitution provides.

Rating: 15 points.

2) Training (maximum 15 points).

She was succeeded by Yitzhak Rabin, another well loved politician, well-seasoned in Israeli politics.

Rating: 10 points.

c. Style (maximum 20 points).

She is still deeply loved today by her people and by millions more throughout the world. Her dedication to her country and her personal concern for all people are legendary. Whatever Golda Meir did, she did for the people. "If Greatness is given a name, it surely is Golda Meir."

Rating: 20 points.

Total Rating: 85 points.

"When we got into office, the thing that surprised me the most was that things were as bad as we'd been saying they were."

"In the final analysis, our most basic common link, is that we all inhabit this small planet, we all breathe the same air, we all cherish our children's futures, and we are all mortal."

JOHN FITZGERALD KENNEDY
1917 - 1963
U.S. Congressman, U.S. Senator, Author
35th President of the United States

John Fitzgerald Kennedy

a. Strategy (maximum 50 points).

JFK had two missions. While he failed to end the Cold War, he faced down the Russians in the Cuban Missile Crisis. Domestically, he had difficulty getting his programs through Congress, although his successor, Lyndon Johnson, after the assassination, got Congress to pass the program.

Rating: 20 points.

b. Succession (maximum 30 points).

1) Process (maximum 15 points).

U. S. Constitution provides.

Rating: 15 points.

2) Training (maximum 15 points).

JFK's relationship with Lyndon Johnson was stronger than most people realized. Both served in the Senate together and were clearly in tune and in touch.

Rating: 15 points.

c. Style (maximum 20 points).

JFK had the magic touch, with wit and charm. The word "charisma" was almost invented for him. Despite his fortune, he appeared to be a man of the people and is still deeply loved today by many.

Rating: 20 points.

Total Rating: 70 points.

I am extraordinarily patient, provided I get my own way in the end.

Europe will never be like America.
Europe is a product of history.
America is a product of philosophy.

MARGARET THATCHER
1925 -
Member of Parliament & Cabinet Secretary
Longest serving Prime Minister of the United
Kingdom

Margaret Thatcher

a. Strategy (maximum 50 points).

As a true conservative, her mandate was to reverse the UK's severe economic decline and to reduce the role of government in economic affairs. Despite intense opposition, she fought successfully for her programs, which did, in fact, turn the situation around. She also refused to cede the Falkland Islands and won the brief war against the Argentineans.

Rating: 45 points.

b. Succession (maximum 30 points).

1) Process (maximum 15 points).

Provided by English law.

Rating: 15 points.

2) Training (maximum 15 points).

Her party was turned out of power in 1990. John Major was the designated successor, but his leadership was largely ineffective.

Rating: 5 points.

c. Style (maximum 20 points).

Thatcher was either loved or hated, depending on the particular situation, but all respected her will and determination. She earned the epithet "The Iron Lady", and wore it with pride.

Rating: 15 points.

Total Rating: 80 points.

"A sense of humor is part of the art of leadership, of getting along with people, of getting things done."

"We succeed only as we identify in life, or in war, or in anything else, a single overriding objective, and make all other considerations bend to that one objective."

DWIGHT DAVID EISENHOWER
1890 - 1969
U. S. General who led the invasion of Europe in WWII
34th President of the United States

Dwight David Eisenhower

a. Strategy (maximum 50 points).

Eisenhower campaigned on the promise to go to Korea and end the war. After his landslide victory, he kept his promise and succeeded. His secondary mission was to get the nation back on a prosperous course. With the institution of the Interstate Highway Program, he ushered in the greatest boom this country has experienced.

Rating: 50 points.

b. Succession (maximum 30 points).

1) Process (maximum 15 points).

Provided by the U.S. Constitution.

Rating: 15 points.

2) Training (maximum 15 points).

He largely kept his Vice President in the dark and did little to continue his administration.

Rating: 0 points.

c. Style (maximum 20 points).

He apparently hated controversy, doing little to protect his chief of staff who was forced to resign for accepting gifts; and of avoiding any comment regarding the rabble-rousing Wisconsin Senator Joseph McCarthy. On the whole, he was well-liked and admired.

Rating: 10 points.

Total Rating: 75 points.

**"I know
of no more encouraging
fact
than the
unquestioned ability
of a man to elevate his life
by conscious endeavor."**

HENRY DAVID THOREAU
(1817 - 1862)
US Transcendentalist Author

Anyone Can Be A Leader

How do you become a leader? Do leaders happen by accident? You can become a leader by accident, without planning for it. But, is it a matter of luck? The answer lies in how you define "luck." If you win the lottery, that's a different kind of luck (some would call it "dumb luck") than being selected to be the leader of a group,

There are two main attributes of luck: preparation and opportunity. Each of us is the beneficiary of thousands upon thousands of opportunities every single day. When we see one that has an appeal, and we are unsuccessful in obtaining it, we typically shrug and cross it off as bad luck.

Most of the time, a missed opportunity is a result of poor preparation. Imagine waking up in the morning and thinking to yourself that today's winning lottery number is 98765. If you fail to prepare yourself by purchasing a ticket with that number, you have missed the opportunity even if you were 100% correct! You could, of course, been 100% sure of winning if you purchase a ticket for every number from 1 to 999,999. You would have become a winner if that was your goal, even though you would have lost money and time in the process. In brief, you would have been fully prepared.

As you can see, being prepared requires a personal investment. In the above example, the time required to purchase a million tickets makes the process prohibitive, much less the cost. If you want to have the luck of being a leader, you need to prepare and to be prepared to expend resources, time and effort to achieve it.

"Always listen to experts.

They'll tell you what can't be done and why.

Then do it."

ROBERT HEINLEIN
1907 - 1988
U. S. Science Fiction Author

You should take heed of the fact that leadership isn't all glory. Leadership has responsibilities, and you may not want those responsibilities on your shoulders. Being President of the United States, for example, has many honors associated with it, but everyone who ever had that job aged far more than normal during his tenure.

Running a business has many rewards, but the businessman or businesswoman of integrity takes on a responsibility for each employee in the organization. If you run a club, you assume a certain degree of responsibility for each member. As a parent, you are the leader of a family, and you take enormous responsibility for each person, particularly for each child.

If you aspire to leadership, be aware that attaining leadership is acquiring responsibility. If you are not willing to accept the responsibility for those who will look to you for guidance; if you are not willing to accept the responsibility for the strategy and planning; then you may be well-advised to become a follower, rather than a leader.

Let's assume that being aware of this, you still aspire to leadership. If you do, that's wonderful. The world needs more and better leaders.

How do **YOU** become an effective leader?

"A man cannot govern a nation if he cannot govern a city;

he cannot govern a city if he cannot govern a family;

he cannot govern a family unless he can govern himself;

and he cannot govern himself unless his passions are subject to reason."

HUGO GROTIUS (Hugo de Groot)
1583 – 1645
Netherlands Jurist
Laid the foundations for International Law
Philosopher, Playwright, Poet

Making Yourself a Leader

If you are reading this book, it would seem that you are interested in becoming a leader or a better leader. Your first requirement is motivation. How motivated are you?

There are many situations where motivation is applied externally. Worried about losing your job? You make certain you arrive early. You work harder. Picture the marine recruit in basic training. The function of the Drill Instructor is to motivate the trainee. In short, every time you are in a situation where the outcome may be unpleasant, you become motivated. Hopefully, for your sake, the motivation is strong enough to make you take action to correct the situation.

Unfortunately, this is not always so. Since the early 1960s, for example, it has been well-publicized that smoking is bad for your health. Yet, in the United States, an estimated 46 million people are still smokers. Despite the well publicized health dangers, the fear of serious illness is simply not strong enough to provide the necessary motivation.

Fear is not the only motivator. There are many reasons for Individuals to be motivated. The strongest motivators for leadership appear to be money, power, and recognition (fame). What motivates you? Why do you want to become a leader? What is your motivation? Unless that motivation is strong enough, you are ultimately doomed to fail. Lack of a strong enough motivation will result in a failure of commitment and self-discipline.

"Your vision will become clear only when you look into your heart.

Who looks outside, dreams.

Who looks inside, awakens."

CARL GUSTAV JUNG
1875 – 1961
Swiss Psychiatrist
Founder of Analytical Psychology.

THREE BIG QUESTIONS

1. Do you really want to be a leader?

2. Whatever your motivation, are you sufficiently motivated to make the commitment necessary to achieve that goal?

3. Are you ready to make that commitment, assume the corresponding responsibilities, and are you capable of the necessary self-discipline to make it happen?

If you cannot honestly answer these questions with a resounding "Yes!" you may want to re-think your leadership ambitions.

WHERE IT STARTS

Leadership of others starts with you! Your first step is to lead yourself. How can you expect others to follow you, if you cannot lead your very own self? One of the prime tools of all leaders is leadership by example. It would seem obvious that you have to demonstrate, on a continuing basis, that you have control over your own life.

"*A winner is someone who recognizes his God-given talents, works his tail off to develop them into skills, and uses these skills to accomplish his goals.*"

LARRY BIRD
1956 –
Boston Celtics Superstar
National Basketball Assn.

Gaining Control Over Your Life

The Vision

You first step in self-leadership is to define (the rest of) your life starting with a "Vision." True, the Vision is only a dream, but it defines your goal or your dream. It is the way you picture in your mind the end result of all your leadership efforts. This Vision is quite naturally followed by a Mission. The Mission is a general outline of what your purposes are and what you expect to achieve. Alexander the Great, for example, had a Vision of being Ruler of the World. This was followed by a mission of conquering each country and bringing them under his umbrella.

It would be helpful to have a vision of where you would like to be ten or twenty years from now, but that is not essential. You can use a period as short as a year. My personal preference is three to four years. Bear in mind, however, that YOUR Vision is not permanent. You should expect to revisit and perhaps revise that Vision as both the world and you change.

If you want to be a leader, this is where it starts. Your vision should include leadership of something. You may want to head a business, a political organization, a club or some social organization. Being a leader is not just believing you have the skill, it is being the leader in some organization.

The Mission

Every organization exists for a reason. That reason is its purpose or mission. When the purpose has been accomplished or no longer valid, the mission must be redefined or the organization will cease to exist. There are many examples in our culture. Organizations devoted to stamping a specific disease either die or redefine themselves when a cure is found.

Many corporations have defined their mission poorly and became victims of technological change. A good example is the U. S. passenger railroad system. Before World War II, rail was the favored method of transportation between cities. Bus companies, Greyhound in particular, offered a cheaper, but less comfortable way to go. Air travel zoomed in popularity after WWII. With government subsidies, it rapidly replaced railroads, and the extensive people transportation by rail network evaporated. Amtrak is something of a revival, but it depends on the whim of politicians for survival. The problem was that the mission was to provide "rail" transportation instead of just transportation. If railroad executives defined their mission as one of moving people by whatever means were most feasible, they perhaps would be the owners of today's airlines. Railroad companies made the same mistake with freight, and lost an enormous amount of business to the trucking industry.

Another example is the Underwood Corporation, once the leading manufacturer of typewriters. Their leadership could not adapt to the technological change to word-processors and computers and was absorbed by Olivetti, the Italian communications giant.

This is why the Mission, your mission, is so important. It is a statement of what you want to do. It is a broad map with many possible avenues toward accomplishing your dream (vision). Do not go past this lightly, because this is where your leadership path begins. Your vision is how you see yourself now and how you picture yourself in the future. Your mission consists of the things you must do to fulfill that future picture.

Defining the mission is more than saying, "I want to be a leader in three years." The more precise you can be, the easier it will be to chart your course. What the mission does is give you a place to aim. You know where you are now. The mission is where you want to be in a certain amount of time. You can be precise or flexible about the length of time.

If you have done this, and admittedly it may take a great deal of introspection to really examine what you are capable of doing, what skills you have, and what skills you will need; you now are in a position to develop Your Life Plan. If your purpose is to be a leader of an organization, your vision and your mission should be directed that way. Having such a goal will enable you to direct your strategy and plans to that end.

Having a clearly defined goal, purpose or mission is necessary for your progress towards becoming a leader. Once you have clarified your Vision and defined your Mission, it is necessary to consider the Three S' of Leadership: Strategy, Succession and Style.

"A goal without a plan is just a wish."

ANTOINE DE SAINT-EXUPERY
1900 - 1944
French Author *The Little Prince*

Strategy

Having a Vision and a Mission is only the beginning. You now have to follow up with a Strategy for achieving that mission. You need to go through the leadership steps, applying each step to your own life. Are you motivated to do this? Are you committed to this? If not, all the advice and examples in the world will not change you. The basis of personal change is to be motivated, to make a commitment and to exercise the self-discipline to make it all happen.

Your first job is to map your strategy. This is the key to the rest of your life, or at least the extent of your vision, and your ascent to leadership. Take plenty of time and do all of the steps. If you are not sure of something, take your best guess and proceed from there. You should ultimately achieve a written plan, a map to follow day-by-day. If nothing else happens, at least you have led yourself!

This process, however, is beneficial in many ways. It forces you to plan, something that hardly anyone does. Lack of planning is a pandemic in the world. People drift aimlessly day after day without any idea of where they are going, what their financial status is, or how they will be able to survive in later years. Are you that type, or will you do better?

In essence, what you need is a personal roadmap to reach your goal. This is an involved undertaking for anyone, but it is even more difficult when you have no idea of your life goals, when you have no idea of what your legacy might be, and when you have not firmly fixed the purpose of your life in your own heart and mind.

*"What do you want
to get done?*

*In what order of
importance?*

Over what period of time?

*What is the time
available?*

*What is the best strategy
for application of time
to projects for the
most effective results?"*

DR. TED W. ENGSTROM
President Emeritus of World Vision
Evangelical Minister
Prolific Author
Editor, *Pursuit of Excellence*

Once you know what your target is, you need to assess your abilities, your character, your strengths and your weaknesses. What skills do you possess that will help you achieve your mission? More importantly, what skills or training do you need to acquire to achieve your purpose?

Your strategy is to outline what steps you have to take to achieve the leadership position you desire. That's fine, but it doesn't go far enough. Suppose, for example, that you have determined you must improve your communication skills. Doing so is part of your strategy. To implement the strategy you need a detailed plan. Will you take a special course in communications? Will you take a public speaking class? Will you join Toastmasters? Planning is the process by which you specify what you are going to do and when to move your strategy along.

The better the plan, the more likely you will succeed. Bear in mind, that until you implement the plan, it is still only a dream. Of all the characteristics of a successful leader, the most important is having the self-discipline to make it work.

There is no magic to this. Every skill you need to acquire takes time, probably more time than you think. Motivational writers seem to agree that it takes at least 1,000 hours to learn any new skill and perhaps ten times that to do it really well. While I believe this is too generalized – it doesn't take 1,000 hours to learn to ride a bicycle – it surely takes more than that to become a skilled engineer.

Your plan is to assess each necessary item in your strategy, and then write down how you intend to accomplish it. This is not just a statement. It includes time, cost and benchmarks. As you implement the plan, you need to be able to look at it any time to see where you stand and how far you have come.

Self analysis is always difficult. One of the things you should consider is finding someone to help you. This person should be someone you trust and whose judgment you respect. The function of this person is NOT to tell you what to do or how to get there. The function is that of a "Mistake Monitor," i.e., a person who will unselfishly and frankly tell you when you are making a mistake.

There have been countless times in my business career where I made a mistake. We all make mistakes, but I'm talking about errors that caused a business to fail. I'm talking about errors where a shift in emphasis would have dramatically changed the results. There are many businesses that made the same classic mistake that I did in one of my ventures. The mistake was allocating 80% of available capital to product development and 20% to marketing.   In retrospect, it should have been the reverse. The net result was that we were "out-marketed" by a competitor with a vastly inferior product.

Even if your plan is wrong or needs modification that should not stop you. The mere presence of a plan puts you far ahead of almost everyone else. With a plan you are no longer drifting. With a plan you have a goal. With a plan you have a way of reaching that goal.

Few people have any plan at all. For them, life is a series of days where they work at jobs they don't particularly enjoy; interspersed with weekends of shopping, parties, cleaning up the house and perhaps watching television. Their finances tend to be messy. Chances are they owe massive amounts on their credit cards for "stuff" they rarely, if ever, use.

Is this really what you want?

If not, formulating a life plan is an answer. Take it one step at a time. Take a pad and jot down what your goals, expectations and hopes are at the age of 80. Eighty is a good cut-off, because the majority of people don't ever get there; and if you reach 80, your plan and your future are pretty much set.

This may take considerable thinking and a considerable amount of time. Don't short cut this step, because everything follows from what you finally decide upon.

Strategy is intertwined with planning. Strategy is much broader, representing the long term overall method to be used in achieving the goal, mission or purpose. In a business or technical organization the long term strategy could be budget allocation, achieving goals in human resource development, or simply maintaining or increasing market share.

Tactics, on the other hand, covers a much shorter period. The tactical plan is what you are going to do today, tomorrow, next week or next month to implement the strategy.

*"He who every morning
plans the transaction
of the day
and follows out that plan,
carries a thread
that will guide him
through the maze
of the most busy life.*

*But where no plan is laid,
where the disposal of time
is surrendered
merely to
the chance of incidence,
chaos will soon reign."*

VICTOR HUGO
1802 – 1885
French Dramatist, Novelist, Poet

Time Management

The biggest drawback to fulfillment of your plan is lack of time. Somehow, there is never enough time to do everything we want to do. Ordinary everyday tasks and responsibilities overwhelm us. "Someday we'll clean the attic!", and someday just never comes. Unfortunately, we develop time-wasting habits where we react to events rather than control what we do. The only way to resolve this particular problem is to take charge of your own life.

One of the most prolific time-wasters today is the screen. Whether it's a TV screen, a cell-phone screen or a computer screen, we sit there and time passes. Are you getting any benefit from this? What could you be doing instead? When the weekend rolls around, do you fix those things around the house that need doing, or do you grab a beer and plunk down on the couch to watch the game?

Preparing your life plan requires time. You need to set aside time every single day to write down your vision, your mission, your strategy and your detailed plan. You need the time to prepare yourself so that you are lucky when the right opportunity comes by.

Leadership skills take time to develop. If you don't have the necessary time, then you have lost the opportunity to decide what you are going to do next, because events will control you instead of the other way around. When you lose control over your time, when you fail to manage your time, you have lost control of your life. You will not be able to complete your Life Plan. You will not be an effective leader, because you will not be able to control your own situation, much less the situation of others.

*"Time is the coin of your life.
It is the only coin you have, and only you can determine how it will be spent.*

Be careful lest you let other people spend it for you."

CARL SANDBURG
1878 - 1967
U. S. Biographer, Poet

Time use requires constant re-evaluation. Sure, you need time with your family. Of course you have to work. The average American watches television 30 hours a week. That's almost as much time as the average American works! This is lost time. You can never regain it. It is robbing you of the opportunity to better yourself. It is preventing you from becoming a leader.

The first step in leadership is to lead yourself. Lead yourself into preparing for the time when you will have attained the status you seek. You need time to prepare your Life Plan. If you follow your Life Plan you know that you are studying what you need to study, you know you are developing your communication skills and you are practicing your leadership skills. If you can do those things, do your regular work properly, spend time with your family and friends and still have time to waste, that's fine.

Time is not only valuable, but it is scarce. It is irreplaceable and cannot be saved for use at a later date. You need to control your time if you are to be a leader. As a leader, you will also be controlling other people's time. Anything of value requires time to create, time to produce, and time to enjoy.

Time is the essential ingredient for every relationship and every endeavor. Take the time to plan your time.

There are two critical principles of time management which you should always bear in mind.

1) A thing, anything takes as long as it takes.

This may sound a bit foolish, but it is very real. The boss gives an instruction to an employee and says he has to have it by 3:00 PM.　Is he asking the impossible?　No matter how loud he screams, if it can't be done in the time given, he can't have it!　In the same way, if you want to develop a specific skill, you have to take the time to do it.　It takes a minimum of 500 hours to do almost anything reasonably well, and in most cases 1,000 hours is probably closer to the mark.　It probably takes ten times that long to become an expert.

If you want to improve your communication skills, one of the best ways is to join Toastmasters.　Yet, even in this organization which emphasizes public speaking (communication) skills and leadership development, If you attend a two-hour meeting every week it will take you five years to gain some proficiency.　In those 500 hours, you will perhaps be fortunate to deliver 50-60 speeches of an average seven minutes in length.　Having observed and been a partaker in this process for more than 15 years, I can testify that every active participant improves, but really good speakers (like anything else) are rare.

2) Hard time drives out soft time.

It is a basic principle of economics (Gresham's Law) that bad money drives out good.　Imagine an economy where counterfeit money is plentiful.　Within a short time, no one will use the good money.　In the same way, if you are working (hard time) it will push out soft time, such as taking your son to the ball game. As a result, failure to plan your time, inevitably results in not being able to do the things you want to do, because hard time, items with higher priority, will take precedence.

Every minute you waste results in a loss of soft time. You, and only you, must decide what your time priorities are. You need to keep in mind what is important to you right now and what is important to you for the future.

The tool of time management permits you to decide on your personal priorities and act upon them. If you have difficulty with this, you might try the Andrew Carnegie system. Andrew Carnegie, at one time considered the richest man in the world, was also one of the first prominent industrialists. He was lavish with his philanthropy and was extremely busy all the time. His system of time management was quite simple. He kept a small notebook in his pocket. At the start of each day he would write down all of the things that he had to do. He then rewrote the list in order of priority! As each thing was done, he would cross it off the list. Meanwhile he would be adding to the bottom of the list. The process was repeated the next day. An assistant once remarked to him "But some things never get done." Andrew replied, "Then they just aren't important enough"

*"The man
who acquires the ability
to take full possession
of his own mind
may take possession
of anything else
to which he is justly
entitled."*

ANDREW CARNEGIE
1835 - 1919
Founder Carnegie Steel Corporation
Founder Carnegie Foundation
U.S. Businessman, Philanthropist

Obstacles to Gaining Control

Imagine you are a salesman of a widely used product. You are in the middle of a sales call. Which of the following do you believe is the most important quality or characteristic for your successful completion of the sale?

1. You are offering the best price.

2. You are offering the best value.

3. Your company has the best reputation for service.

4. You have complete product knowledge and can intelligently answer any question about the product or your company.

5. Your company can deliver the product faster than any competitor.

6. You have excellent persuasive ability.

7. You are enthusiastic about your company and the product.

8. The prospect was referred to you by a friend.

9. The prospect has previously used your company's products.

10. The customer is gullible.

While all may be important, the most universal answer among sales experts is answer number seven. More important than any other factor is the attitude of the sales person. Consistently, customers want to feel comfortable doing business with some one. Here's an old fable to illustrate the point.

A man and his young son were hiking in the mountains, when all of a sudden, the boy tripped and fell. "Ouch", he cried loudly. An echo came back, "Ouch!" The boy looked around and yelled, "Who are you?" The echo came back, "Who are you?" The boy, hurt and angered by the response yelled out, "You are stupid!" The echo came back "You are stupid!" The boy, utterly frustrated, screamed "I hate you!" Once again the echo came back, "I hate you!"

After that the father said to his son, "You're not doing this the proper way. Watch me." With that, the father cupped his hands around his mouth like a megaphone and shouted "Hello!" The answer came back, and the father then shouted "I like you!" Once again, the same answer came back. The father then shouted "You're a champion!" and the answer, of course, repeated what the man had shouted.

"Son," the father said, "What you heard was Echo, the spirit of the mountain. What Echo teaches us is that whatever we give, we get back. If you smile, you will get a smile back. If you frown, you will get a frown back. If you are pleasant to others, others will be pleasant to you. If you are nasty, others will be nasty to you. If you give cheerfulness, you will receive cheerfulness. Best of all, if you give love, you will get love in return."

As a salesman or as a leader, you simply must have the right attitude. You cannot afford to be pessimistic. You can't afford to take a position of negativism. If you whine, complain or evince a sour attitude, you will not be able to inspire others or have them follow your lead. Just as in the story, your world has the spirit of Echo. If you expect to be a successful leader, you must deal from a position of cheerfulness, optimism and goodwill. This attitude of cheerfulness is a necessity not only for the successful salesperson, but for the successful leader as well. Sometimes it pays other dividends, too.

Fifty years ago, as I was starting my computer systems career, I went to work for a manufacturing company. My office was on the eighth floor and the company cafeteria was on the second. The job was a significant step up for me in every way including salary. About three weeks after I started, after lunch, going back to my office one day, I was stopped by an elderly gentleman as I was getting off the elevator. "What's your name." he asked me. I told him. "Who is your boss?' he queried. I told him, smiled and went on my way. A half hour later, my boss called me into his office. He said, "Did you meet M.V. on the elevator?" "Who is M. V.?", I asked. My boss replied, "He's the Chairman of the Board, and he just instructed me to give you a raise, because he likes to have happy people in the company, and he said you smile all the time."

Who ever said "It hurts to smile?"

*"The optimist
proclaims that we live
in the best
of all possible worlds;
and the pessimist
fears this is true."*

JAMES BRANCH CABELL
1879 – 1958
U. S. Essayist, Novelist

Becoming an Effective Leader

If you make a commitment to follow the steps we have outlined, and if you keep that commitment, I guarantee that you will become a leader. Maybe not in the place you were aiming for, but somewhere. Why? Simply because there are so few good leaders available!

Look around you. Look at a few of our so-called leaders. Are they effective? Do you want to go where they lead? Every day, it seems, television, radio and the newspapers unearth some situation where a leader is corrupt, careless, criminal or incompetent. Over the past ten years we have had case after case of ineffective leadership in business, in the schools, in charitable institutions, in government and, heaven help us, even among the clergy.

The world is crying for leadership. Are you ready to play your part? Here's what you have to do.

Follow the steps carefully through the Vision, Mission, Strategy and Planning steps. Then dare to make a commitment to follow through. This is not like the typical New Year's resolution which lasts a few days. This is a lifetime commitment. You've got to be absolutely committed to the process. You will be a leader. It's the difference between the chicken and the pig. When you sit down to a bacon and eggs breakfast; the chicken is involved, but the pig is committed.

Many of us are aware of others who have obtained fancy job titles, but are leaders in name only. As the old saying goes, They want the fame but aren't willing to play the game." If this is your goal, you are wasting your time reading this book. You need to make a commitment to excellence. If you have any doubt what that is, I suggest you read either one of Tom Peters excellent books: *In Search of Excellence* or *The Book of WOW!*. What these two positive works emphasize is that leadership and excellence just do not happen. It takes time, effort and resources. If you watch the incredible performances of Olympic athletes, you cannot help being amazed at the feats they perform. Yet, most of us are not really aware of the dedication this takes of training and practice for hours every day, every week, for years and years. That's commitment, self-discipline, and hard work all together. For you to have that kind of success, you not only need the commitment, but you have to spend the time. Even if you do these things, it will not guarantee your success. I practiced swimming three hours a day, every day, for years, and still didn't make the team, because I simply was not fast enough.

Even if you do all of the positive things outlined in this book, you may not become an effective leader. Effectiveness as a leader goes beyond everyday levels, because it requires two very specific qualities possessed only by truly great leaders: ability to make a decision, and the power of innovation.

Ability To Make A Decision

An effective leader must be prepared, even in the most stressful circumstances, to make a decision. This is not to advocate micro-management. It's the big decisions that are meaningful. As the comedian, Henny Youngman, used to say *"In my house I make the big decisions and my wife makes all the small ones. She decides where we go on vacation, what kind of a car we'll buy and how much to spend on a house. I decide the big things: should the United States go to war and should we increase Social Security taxes."*

The decision-making process for many is extremely difficult. Regardless of how carefully you analyze, there is always the possibility that you decided incorrectly. Even worse, is the <u>unconscious decision not to make a decision</u>! If you have difficulty making decisions, you will have difficulty becoming an effective leader.

You can overcome your fears of decision making with practice. Start with small things and small decisions. If you usually put your left shoe on first, make a decision and put the right shoe on first for the next three days. Go back to the other foot for a day and then go back to putting on the wrong shoe first again. Every day, you put the wrong shoe on first, you are making a conscious decision. Do you have the same thing every day for breakfast? Tomorrow morning, have something entirely different. Change again the following day.

What this procedure does is force you to make a conscious decision. In every part of your life, you become used to doing things a certain way. When faced with something new, if you have trouble with decision making, you have no anchor. You have not had the experience of making a previous decision about the same thing.

You are in the habit of assuming that the outcome of a decision will be exactly the same as the outcome of a similar previous situation. The fact is that there are probably differences you have not considered. The prime rule of decision making is to examine the facts and consider all the alternatives you can.

Faced with a making a decision means avoiding common traps. You need to be sure that you have all of the facts available. You also need to be sure that you are not making invalid assumptions. The fear of making the wrong decision is largely based on being proved wrong <u>after the fact.</u> Monday morning quarterbacking serves no purpose.

If you make a bad or a poor decision, learn to live with it!   You will make many mistakes over your lifetime. EVERYBODY DOES! The important thing is that you get in the habit of making decisions. Even if you flip a coin, you will be right half the time. As you continue to make decisions, you will start to learn how to avoid errors. You will learn to evaluate the quality of the information on which you based your choice.

Sometimes you are forced to make a decision when you don't have all of the facts. In fact, you hardly ever have all the facts at the time you need to make that decision.   This is well recognized in the world of philosophy, dating back to Aristotle in 350 B.C. Theologians and philosophers wrestled with this problem for centuries.   In the fourteenth century, an English logician and Franciscan friar William of Ockham, theorized that the explanation of any phenomenon, hypothesis, theory or decision is most sound when it is based on the fewest number of assumptions. This principle is known as Occam's Razor.

In a similar fashion, statisticians developed Bay's Theorem as a tool to improve probability decisions. Bay's Theorem came into prominence during WWII when the need for improved statistical quality control became necessary for war production. The concept behind Bay's is that in the absence of facts, you should select the most likely answer and assume it is true. For example take the following problem:

If you have a million coins where one coin has heads on both sides, and you pick one coin randomly, then flip it twenty times and it comes up heads every one of the twenty flips, what is the probability you drew the ONLY two headed coin? The answer, applying Bay's Theorem, is one in a million.

You can apply both of these principles to decision making. In fact, most of us do. If you are driving and are approaching a railroad crossing and the red train warning lights begin to flash, do you stop? Do you stop even if you don't hear or see the train? Using Occam's Razor, the simplest explanation is that a train is coming. Bay's Theorem indicates that the highest probability is that an approaching train caused the lights to flash.

In real life we are not so fortunate to have flashing red lights to warn us from making a poor decision. Nevertheless, the principle is clear. It is rare occurrence when you have all the facts. If this is so, then it is rare when you can know everything you should know before making a decision.

A leader is one who knows the way, goes the way, and shows the way.

Dr. JOHN C. MAXWELL
1950 -
U. S. Pastor, Author, Speaker, Leadership Expert
Founder of The Injoy Group
The 21 Irrefutable Laws of Leadership

The effective leader sets forth to gather as much information about a situation as he can reasonably absorb in the time frame allotted. He/she then reviews the information, and then applying both Occam's Razor and Bay's Theorem makes a decision and moves on. If the decision was wrong, it most likely was either misinformation or a lack of information. In either case, the effective leader accepts the fact that a mistake was made. Examination of the reasons why the information was not better and the application of corrective measures might be indicated, but <u>there is nothing that can change the bad decision</u>.

One of the major differences between the truly effective leader and the run-of-the-mill leader is the ability to move on. The effective leader assesses the damage, takes corrective action, but rarely attempts to blame anyone. Blaming a particular person for a bad decision is an exercise in stupidity. If some one failed to do a job, then corrective action can be taken. The effective leader recognizes that in any analysis, no matter who made the decision, it is the responsibility of the leader.

Paul J. Spiewak

*"Millions of men
have lived to fight,
build palaces
and boundaries,
shape destinies
and societies;
but the compelling force
of all times
has been the force of
originality and creation
profoundly affecting
the roots of human spirit."*

ANSEL ADAMS
1902-1984
Renowned Photographer & Conservationist

Innovation

Innovation is an essential ingredient of effectiveness. A leader who simply continues in the same fashion fails in fulfilling the mission. The reason is that there is always a loss along the way. Engineers attribute this loss to "friction." In Las Vegas, they say that "the house always takes a cut." Whatever the endeavor, whatever the organization, there is always attrition of some kind. Every businessman knows that he will lose some of his customers. To be successful, he takes steps to add new customers to replace those that leave. Every club loses members, and almost every club has a method of getting new members.

Whatever the situation, each organization must be able to progress toward the fulfillment of its purpose by innovation. Individuals also need to innovate. Admittedly some are better at it than others, but everyone, almost every day makes some kind of innovation. If you can't find a potholder, you use a towel or a shirt. If you are thirsty and there is no water, you drink a beer or a soda. This classic story tells it best.

A man driving along the road gets a flat tire. He pulls to the side of the road and prepares to change the tire. He jacks up the car, removes the wheel with the flat, carefully placing the lug nuts into the removed hubcap on the ground. He removes the spare from the trunk, places the wheel with the flat in the trunk, closes the trunk, and rolls the spare toward the newly emptied wheel. As he gets near, the spare hits the hubcap, overturns it and all of the lug nuts go down a storm drain. Standing there, scratching his head, wondering what to do, he glances up and sees that he is parked in front of a mental institution.

An inmate is watching him from an open window and shouts to him, "Why don't you take a lug nut from each of the other wheels and then drive to a station where you can replace the missing ones?" The driver smiles and says, "That's a great idea. What's a smart fellow like you doing in a mental institution?" The inmate replies "I may be crazy, but I'm not stupid."

Most people resist change. There is a level of comfort in doing things the same way, even when we know that we can improve. The ability to innovate is inherent in the quality we call "Leadership." It is a tragedy that so few people can apply that ability in unexpected situations. The great majority want things to stay the way they always were rather than search for new or better ways. The degree of resistance to change is incredible. People go to unbelievable lengths to avoid changing the way something is done, even if it has been done in an inefficient or unintelligent way for years.

Here is an example from personal experience.

A number of years ago, as a new manager of a company facing bankruptcy, my immediate focus was to reduce costs and to improve efficiency. The first day, I watched the office procedure to enter the prior day deliveries. Delivery slips were sorted alphabetically. Then, an alphabetic file was searched to locate the correct customer number which was then written on the delivery slip. After completing this process, the slips were then sorted by customer number, brought to the ledger clerk. The ledger clerk, who carefully kept the ledgers in customer number sequence, would then post the charges on each customer's ledger.

The same process was used for posting checks. After sorting checks alphabetically, the customer number was researched and then written on the check. The checks were resorted by customer number and delivered to the posting clerk who then posted the payments.

STOP! A little bit of thought on the process is a just cause for scratching one's head. "Why not", I asked myself, "re-sort the ledger cards in alphabetical order. Then post the deliveries and checks after they have been sorted alphabetically and post." This would eliminate the need for customer number research, allow for removal of the customer number cross files, and the resorting of all items by customer number. The result would be a saving of one employee.

I announced that, "Starting tomorrow, we would do away with customer numbers. Henceforth we would post and control customers alphabetically." I was attacked immediately as "being an idiot", "not understanding how an office worked", "sabotaging the company" etc. I stood my ground. The service manager threatened to quit. The bookkeeper went to the boss and told him that the whole business would fall apart without customer numbers, and that if I was permitted to go ahead with it, he would quit. Further, he added, that he would be "expecting a huge bonus when they called him back to straighten the mess out."

I stood firm, explaining why my way was better. I won the point, but was warned that my job was "on the line" and if the new way failed, I would be fired. The result was a much smoother, faster operation with less work. The bookkeeper, unbeknown to me at the time, was a relative of my boss' partner, who resented my presence until he received the next Profit & Loss Statement.

In another personal situation, the company was having a great deal of trouble matching production to sales. The sales department was constantly complaining (and rightfully so) that there was too long a delay in shipping individual items. The manufacturing department was maintained that it was not their fault, because they were manufacturing items in response to the product sales reported to them by the sales department. As the company "troubleshooter", one day I witnessed a classic confrontation. The Vice President of Sales, jumped out of his chair, slammed his hand on the desk and shouted, "Why the H--- can't you make the "*&%$*!" junk we can sell, not the "*&%$*!" junk we can't sell?" The Vice President of Manufacturing responded instantly. He jumped out of his chair, slammed his hand on the desk, and shouted, "Why the H--- can't you sell the "*&%$*!" junk we can make, not the "*&%$*!" junk we can't make? This particular situation had been festering for quite some time. It was obvious, at least to me, that something was wrong with the data or the procedures. The answer proved to be that the "sales" figures were based on "shipments" rather than "orders." As a result, all of the previous production and inventory errors, and the past shipping delays were being perpetuated. Even when this was pointed out, it took almost a full year to get agreement to change the procedure and to report "orders" rather than "shipments."

Innovation is the life blood of every organization. An effective leader must be an innovator. Whether it is a business, a charitable organization, a foundation, a social organization, or a political one, the effective leader constantly searches for ways to improve the functioning of the organization.

Leadership Training

If you search the Internet on the subject of Leadership Training, you will find more than a quarter of a billion entries. Obviously, no one can hope to examine all of these choices and still have time left for a career.

In general, they break down into a few main categories. These are:

1. Business and management skills.

2. Human resource skills.

3. Technical skills, especially relating to use of computers.

4. Time Management.

5. Communication.

6. Decision making .

A sampling indicated that very few of these training opportunities deal with the philosophy of leadership. Most seem to dwell on the technical skills needed to be a leader, avoiding definitions of a Vision or of a Mission. Yet these factors are at the heart of any organization seeking effective leadership.

Nowhere could I find any mention of "Succession" considerations as a necessary requirement for effective leadership. Yet, no matter the type of organization, succession is a major consideration.

Thousands of new small businesses are formed on a daily basis. Almost all of these are subject to immediate failure if the main person becomes indisposed. Hardly any of these has a clearly defined Vision or Mission, much less a strategy for fulfilling the Mission.

Too many small businesses exist where the owner keeps the business plan "under his hat." This is not Leadership, it is <u>leadership failure</u>. A business lacking leadership will not necessarily fail, but if there is intelligent competition, it will be hard put to survive. Such instances are not rare, but when conditions change, these businesses suffer.

On a larger scale, most business have neither a clearly defined mission nor a business plan. Whether this is a matter of laziness or ignorance, it is a failure of leadership.

In summary, this book is a layman's book about the Philosophy of Leadership. When you approach the subject of leadership, it is apparent that some people are more suited to be leaders than others. We all know this. As we grow up, we recognize that there are people who seem to have a natural talent for leadership. They become the class officers in school. They become captains of athletic teams. They become club officers.

In any voluntary organization or club, it always seems as if there is a small cadre of people who do all the work. This core, of perhaps no more than four or five people, is critical to the continued functioning of the organization. The members of this core group are the true leaders, even though others may claim titles and glory. Without that core, there would be nothing to lead.

Is there some way we can test for future leaders? At what age can we test? The psychologist Walter Mischel, while at Stanford University. devised the "Marshmallow

Test" for this very purpose. The test is applied to children at the age of four. A marshmallow is placed in front of the child, and the child is told "Before we start, I have to do something down the hall. You can eat the marshmallow while I'm gone, but if you wait until I get back, and don't take the marshmallow, I'll give you two marshmallows." Hundreds of children were tested and tracked. Fourteen years later, those who had waited for the two marshmallows appeared to have the habits of successful people. Those who ate the single marshmallow had short attention spans and appeared to be oblivious to long-term considerations.

According to researcher Ronald Gross, an associate of Walter Mischel, the marshmallow test continues in adult life. The desire to please everyone, for example, is a manager "marshmallow" who is forever "interrupt driven." The leader who concentrates on maintaining the current "cash flow" and fails to invest in research, new models or business improvements is another example of "marshmallow" thinking. Indeed, "marshmallow" operational technique seems to be rampant on Wall Street where long term profitability of a company is usually overshadowed by the performance of the last thirteen weeks.

While there are both short term and long term goals, the strategy of the leader must take into account the possible sacrifice of the short term goal, in favor of the long term goal, because the long term goal is the fulfillment of the mission. Fulfilling the mission is the first duty of the effective leader.

Hide not your talents.

They for use were made.

What's a sundial in the shade?"

BENJAMIN FRANKLIN
1706-1790
U. S. Printer, Publisher, Author, Philanthropist,
Statesman

Biting the Bullet

At the beginning of this book, the purpose of "leadership" was defined as "to lead." Coming full circle, if you were asked, "How do you become a leader?" The answer is the same: "Lead."

You can't learn to ride a bicycle, swim, sail a boat, become a good speaker or become a great surgeon by observation. You can't learn to be an effective leader by observation either. The only way to become an effective leader is through practice. If this is your goal, then your first step is to consider ways in which you can start leading. It is only through practice of the art of leadership, that one can develop the qualities of effective leadership.

As pointed out earlier, you have to start with yourself. If you can't lead your own life, how do you expect to lead others? You need to prepare a written strategy and plan for your own life. This will lead you in the proper direction.

The second step is to act like a leader in your daily work. It makes no difference whether you are the head of a major corporation or a farmer. It makes no difference whether you are an automobile mechanic or the foreman in an assembly plant. Whatever your vocation, you need to create a vision of what that position could be at its best. Then you need to define your mission in how to achieve that vision in that job. Then you have to translate that vision into a strategy, followed by a step-by-step operational procedure to achieve that vision. Finally, you must apply yourself to the operating conditions, executing your plan to complete the mission as you have defined it!

There's much more that you can do. One of the most effective ways to develop your leadership skills is to join a club. If you have the time and the inclination join several. After you are in the club, you will learn that there are one or two jobs that nobody seems to want. In some clubs, nobody really wants to be the president! Take the highest job you can find that's available. Volunteer!

There are several good reasons for this. First, you will be more appreciated by the other members, and they will be more likely to follow you and take your suggestions. Nobody wants to lose the guys who are actually doing the work.   Second, each job you assume will give you another opportunity to exercise your leadership skills. Write down your vision of the job. Define your mission. Plan your strategy and <u>write down your plan.</u> As you are doing this, look around for someone who can takeover whatever you started. Remember the second attribute of a good leader is finding and training a successor. Work your plan, find and train your successor and then, go after the next job up the line.

You will be polishing your skills all along the way. Perhaps the best club you could join is Toastmasters International. With more than 10,000 clubs worldwide, almost every community has at least one club. This organization is inexpensive and offers a tremendous range of opportunities both in communication and in leadership.

As you move into more and more clubs, and higher and higher jobs, you will find that this will be occurring in your regular job and within your family. When this happens, you are truly becoming an effective leader.

Quotation Index by Author

Author's Background

This brief biography is provided to make the reader aware of my background and to better understand the material being presented. Because my path has often been that of a maverick, points of view expressed in this book, may be startling. As a product of my experiences: 48 employment situations, 19 entrepreneurial arrangements, founder of more than a dozen companies, leader of more than eight social organizations. I believe I am in a unique position to assess the meaning and measurement of leadership.

The stories, as opposed to fable that are included are taken directly from personal experience, as incredible as it may seem to the reader. This is a book about philosophy, not a guide for dummies, nor is it a checklist.

I was fortunate to grow up in an entrepreneurial atmosphere. My father was in partnership with two of his brothers and his father in a small firm manufacturing men's outerwear. As a child I heard the story repeatedly how my father's father came to this country in 1908 with hardly any assets, but managed to create a small profitable business making sheepskin vests.

Not only was he successful in his own right, but over the course of the years, he helped many related to our family in setting up similar businesses. Indeed, he even helped his brother set up a firm which produced the premier line of "Ladies' & Gentlemen's Leather Automobile Clothing." At the time I graduated high school, there were six such firms, all friendly competitors, in the same business.

Taking advantage of rapid advance options and summer school, I graduated high school at the age of 16, immediately went to college and graduated with a Business degree, just before entering service with the U.S. Army in WWII. I was no great shakes (nor did I want to be) in the Army, as once the war was over, my objective was to get out and enter the business world.

Jobs were scarce in those days (1947). I took a job with my father's firm, working my way through all the factory jobs. After my father retired in 1948, there was no longer a logical place for me in the firm. Having no better prospects, my brother and I opened a retail store. I quickly realized that retailing was not what I wanted to do, and I looked for something else. I became a real estate broker, and soon learned that this was not suited to my personality either. I continued to flounder. I searched the want ads and finally managed to get a rather low-paying job as a degree day clerk in a fuel oil distribution firm. After a year, during which I tried to learn as much as I could about the industry, I moved to another company as the general manager. This new employer was on the verge of bankruptcy and was a fantastic training ground. It was here that my first real taste of leadership began. It was the place where I learned that I had a talent for systems design. Using that talent, we managed to move the company from poverty to prosperity in only two years.

By 1952, it became evident to me, that this, as good as I was in the position, was not where I wanted to spend my life. At that point, my wife and I agreed that the only solution was to get further education. My dream was an M.S. in Engineering, and after attending four different universities, over a seven-year period, at night, I received my long sought degree in 1959.

That degree changed my life! In 1954, one of my professors talked eloquently about the future of data processing. My familiarity with data processing was fairly extensive though it was all pre-computer. My father had installed an elementary punched card system in 1939, which provided me week-end employment. At college, I landed a part-time job in a punched card installation. My last days in the Army were spent in an MRU (Machine Records Unit) where we maintained files by updating the daily "Morning Reports" from each unit in the 1st Army. At the University, I had the opportunity to learn to program the IBM 650 computer, one of the earliest commercial units. I was hooked! Other classes afforded the opportunity to learn Fortran II, one of the early "higher level" programming languages. Over the next 30 years I would learn more than 49 operating systems and computer languages; design more than 100 software systems, both generalized and specific; and offer consulting data processing consulting services to hundreds of customers.

Immediately upon graduation, I received many offers and accepted a position where I was made responsible for improving inventory turnover. The project was fascinating and, over the next four years, I became adept at designing systems of sales forecasting, programming several computers, and controlling inventory and factory production. Along the way, I received recognition for my work by being elected as an officer of the American Production & Inventory Control Society.

Subsequently, I set up the first major data processing consulting company in New York, became first an independent consultant, and then a partner in a data processing service bureau which went public in 1968. As a Vice President in charge of one of the four company divisions, I created the first (and I believe best) system for legal accounting. At that time there were more than 5,000 lawyers, mostly in the New York City Metropolitan Area), including 12 of the 20 largest law firms in the world, using this system which I had designed and implemented. In 1972, I cashed in my stock options and left the company.

Conveniently, I went back into consulting, first as a minor partner in a four-man firm, later as an independent, and then as a full partner with another consultant. In between, I did a stint as a law office administrator, then as an entrepreneur in the vending business. From there I became an individual consultant to one of the Fortune 500 companies, officially became a venture manager for them, and after another two years, left after successful completion of the venture.

In 1978, I started a computer business, both hardware and software, and ran that business until my retirement in 1991. Looking for something to keep me busy, rather than sitting around the condo swimming pool talking about laxatives, I formed THE Reunion Network, Inc. (TRN) to help military reunion planners. I joined Toastmasters in the same year, and have been an active participant in that organization since that time.

It was in this period of fifteen years that I truly became aware of what the differences were between good leaders and bad ones. In the course of those years, my stake in the company grew from a small percent to one of majority control over all operations. Gaining control in 1999, and with the help of Toastmaster tools, the business has tripled in seven years.

In many ways, some people still think of me as an "oddball." Over the years I have done things that most people think as "dare devil" or overly ambitious. For example, our family built an entire house at the end of a mile-and-a-half dirt road in the middle of the woods,

Always oriented toward water sports, I learned to swim at the age of four, and to sail at the age of eleven. I love sailing, but was forced to give it up due to shoulder and elbow problems. I learned to fly an airplane, was certified to fly at night and later in aerobatics. When physical problems forced me, I gave up flying, but then learned to scuba dive. I hold a PADI Master Diver's card and to celebrate my 80th birthday went diving with the sharks in French Polynesia.

In every area, I have tried to advance to the best of my ability. If I joined an organization, my goal was to excel and become a leader. My position titles include: Master of my Masonic Lodge; Commander of Miami Beach Power Squadron; District 8 Lieutenant Commander, United States Power Squadrons, Life Member United States Power Squadrons, President South Florida Navigators Club, Life Member South Florida Navigators Club, President Pembroke Pines Toastmasters Club, Area 23 Governor Toastmasters International, Division E Governor, District 47 Toastmasters International, and President Lake Oscawana Homeowners Assn.

As a seasoned member of Toastmasters and their philosophy of evaluation, I welcome all comments regarding the style, organization and information presented. Send your comments to:
paul@reunionfriendly.com
Hollywood, Florida
November 2006

www.ingramcontent.com/pod-product-compliance
Lightning Source LLC
Chambersburg PA
CBHW061300280526
45784CB00002B/833